The Young Woman and her Self-Esteem

and her

Anita Canfield

Deseret Book Company
Salt Lake City, Utah

For Jason, Ashley, Chase, and Paige, my beautiful sons and
daughters. There are many words to express my Joy
at being your mother here on earth.

But there are no words to tell you of my Joy at the thought
of being your sister forever and throughout eternity!

© 1983 Randall Book Company
© 1990 Anita Canfield

ISBN 0-87579-365-7

Printed in the United States of America   8006

10   9   8   7

JOY

An eighteen-year-old Latter-day Saint girl, whom I will call Linda, sat in my living room and wept bitterly. She recounted the past weeks, months, and years of struggle, trial, and disappointment, and her heart was aching. She came to talk because she could no longer carry the fatigue, loneliness, and sorrow alone. She was at the lowest point in her life, and she knew it. She had no self-respect, no self-esteem, and felt so discouraged.

Her struggles and trials and disappointments had been like those of most young women who begin around age thirteen to stretch into womanhood. The "Lack Of's" in her life seemed exaggerated by the achievements of others, including family and friends around her:

- She had to wear braces on her teeth until she was fifteen.
- She had to save months of babysitting money to be able to afford to buy one pair of designer jeans. Her parents could not afford to buy her the latest clothes.
- She was shy about making new friends.
- Her complexion was less than flawless.
- She struggled to keep up her math grades.
- She didn't get asked to the junior prom.

- She made some mistakes morally.
- She had confrontations with her parents.
- Her father criticized her often and pointed out her faults.
- She withdrew from her parents at times.
- She often said the wrong thing.
- She felt rules were "holding her back."
- She didn't make the swim team.
- She wondered about and was puzzled by some gospel principles.

Linda could see during the past years that she did have some good points, but why couldn't she be as pretty, popular, talented, and well dressed as so many others around her?

This day she came to see me, she was puzzled and confused. She said:

> Anita, all these years of growing up and going to church and living in this world have taught me great sorrow. I have no joy in life. I find myself overwhelmed with three questions and with no self-esteem to proceed.
>
> 1. What do I want in life?
>   Should I go to college, or gain a skill? Do I have any special gifts or talents? Where do I go from here?
>
> 2. Who will I marry?
>   Should I just hang around home and look for marriage? Should I go to school and look for marriage? What will he be like? Should I look for a 'Mr. Perfect?' How will I know the right one?
>
> 3. How can I gain a testimony?
>   My testimony is so weak. I thought it was supposed to be more than it is by age 18. How do I believe and keep going when there is so much disappointment in life?
>
> Anita, I find myself tired and discouraged. I would love to wake up in the morning and be glad to see the day! To wake up and feel joy! But instead I wake up more unhappy every day.

I knew what she was saying, this sweet young friend of mine, because those were once my thoughts too. "Oh! If I could only feel joy in my heart, love myself, and be glad for the challenges of life." I, too, had that overwhelming loneliness of standing at the edge of womanhood and feeling like a stranger looking in.

I wanted to help her so much, and that is exactly how I feel about *you* as I write to *you*, personally and individually. I have two daughters of my own, and what I want to share with you are the things I share with them and nothing less. For you see, more important than being my daughters, they are first my sisters! And so are you. We are part of the family of God. It would be wrong for me to want more for them than for you. This book, then, must be a labor of love, from one sister to another. Mortal life may separate us by a few years, but before this earth life, we were sisters, side by side, and twenty earthly years can never change that!

Even as I ached to help Linda find joy again in being alive, despite disappointments, so I am eager to help you understand joy, too.

When you love yourself, when you feel good about yourself, when you can *accept* yourself, you feel joy! When you reach a goal after planning and working for it, you feel joy! When you bask in the praise of others for your good works, you feel joy! When you get the grades you worked for, you feel joy. When that special date happens, you feel joy. When you feel close to Heavenly Father, you feel joy. And the list goes on and on, and that's what this book is about—joy!

If you were to describe self-esteem in one clear and simple picture, it would be the power-packed little word joy!

I believe we came to earth to learn about things like joy and self-esteem. I know we *wanted* to come here to learn. As we discussed these plans with our Heavenly Father, He told us it wouldn't be easy. He said that there would have to be sorrow, too, because without opposition you cannot understand joy. We might have been a little worried about that. After all, we knew Satan and how ugly he really was. We might have been worried about Satan's ability to tempt and discourage us. I'll bet we discussed that with Father, too.

And being the kind, wise Father that He is, do you know what He did to comfort and reassure us? He promised that He would give us clear guidelines to follow. He promised to send us a roadmap with the right roads clearly marked. He promised. He told us that we would be able to find the ways to know who we are, why we are here, and where we are going. He said we would *definitely* be able to find joy and peace and self-esteem in this life!

If you do not believe that, then you do not believe in who you are! You do not know with all of your heart that you are Heavenly Father's daughter and that He loves you and wants you to return home. He really does. I know that.

But you know, dear friends, it wasn't all that long ago that I wasn't really sure about that.

When I was twelve years old, I remember sitting in a sacrament meeting and hearing the speaker talk about his weaknesses and imperfections. He made it very clear he didn't think he was going to make it to the Celestial Kingdom.

I left that meeting thinking that the Celestial Kingdom was not for ordinary people like me. It was only for super people like bishops and Relief Society presidents. And I am sorry to say I believed that until I was well into my twenties.

Then one day, I realized, "That kind of thinking has no place in the Church of Jesus Christ!" The Celestial Kingdom will be made up of people who are ordinary in an earthly sense but extraordinary in a spiritual sense, because anyone who has God for a Father is not ordinary. They are extra-ordinary because they have one special ability—*they have eternal perspective.*

What on earth is eternal perspective?

There is an old legend about a man named William Faust who lived in Germany in the sixteenth century. Faust was what the world might call an extraordinary person. During his teens he found he had a knack for creating and building businesses. At a very young age he was already a successful and rich person. But that wasn't good enough for Faust; he wanted more! In fact, he wanted all he could get—whatever that meant.

And so, at age 25, he made a deal with the devil. He promised that if Satan would aid him in becoming rich and powerful, in 25 years he would give Satan his soul. Satan agreed, and so began the bargain. For 25 years the devil aided Faust by overpowering his competitors, squelching his enemies, and delivering him all the treasures and power possible. Faust became the fiercest, richest, and most powerful man in Germany. He got everything he wanted; everything he desired. Satan was his servant.

Now when Faust had made his deal, 25 years seemed like it would never come. At age 25, 25 years was a whole lifetime away for Faust. (When you are sixteen, four years seems like such a long time because it is one-fourth of your age; however, four years to a person 40 years old is only one-tenth of their age and doesn't seem long at all!)

Well, time marched on, and the final day of the bargain had come. All day Faust tried to revoke the bargain, but the devil would not consider it. A deal was a deal. Satan had done his part, and the hour had come for Faust to deliver up his soul.

That last hour was a horrible sight to behold. Faust cried and groaned and moaned from deep within his spirit. He wept buckets of tears and cried out in agony. Great beads of sweat soaked his hair and clothing. Back and forth, back and forth he paced the floor, wringing his hands, twisting them, watching the seconds of the clock tick by. Finally, as the stroke of midnight sounded, you could hear his blood curdling scream, "Faust has gone to hell!"

What a dreadful scene. But if Faust could have seen his last hour first, do you think he would have made the bargain? If he could have lived his last hour first, do you think he would have wanted power and riches enough to make such a bargain? I think not.

You see, what Faust lacked was eternal perspective—the ability to see the whole picture, not part of it. The ability to see himself in the future.

If you want to be Celestial Kingdom material and be extraordinary, you must have the ability to see the whole picture. You must be able to see yourself in the pre-existence as a daughter of Father and Mother in Heaven. You must be able to see yourself in the part of our lives yet to come, living again with Father and Mother in Heaven. That is eternal perspective.

And what will having eternal perspective do for you?

When I was in my late twenties and single, I was presented with an interesting opportunity. If I had allowed myself to compromise my standards, I would have had a lot of worldly excitement and material gain. In other words, I would have had a lot of temporary pleasures. But if I had compromised my standards, today I would be a sorrowful person. I didn't know that then. What prevented me from participating in that wickedness was my eternal perspective. I could picture who I was before I came here, who I am now and why I am here on earth, and who I can be in the future and where I want to go from here.

That isn't the only time I have needed eternal perspective. I find that I must hang on to that vision *every* day of my life, every moment that I live, because Satan is often on my back trying to tell me that I'm not extraordinary just because I'm the daughter of God. He will try to destroy us by destroying our eternal perspective. If you lose the vision of that, what will keep you from sin? How will you ever get home?

Now, how do you get eternal perspective? Two simple ways:

1. Have a vision. Yes, you can have a vision. It is the same one I have. I picture myself, dressed in the most beautiful white gown, made of exquisite fabric, covered in laces and pearls. I picture myself in this long, white, flowing gown with a beautiful light all around me. I am standing in the midst of other people, friends, and family who are all in white, and their faces are glowing, too. And there we are surrounding a throne where Father and Mother sit. That vision can be as vivid as I want it to be. And deeply concentrating on it has kept me out of dangerous

water, whether from temptation or from Satan's subtle words to me. That vision is helping me to save myself. That vision brings me joy!

2. The second way to gain eternal perspective is to remember what Father said about giving us the roadmap with the roads clearly marked. You will find the roadmaps in the scriptures. In the scriptures you will find eternal perspective.

I testify to you that eternal perspective brings self-esteem and self-esteem brings joy. In this book I want to share with you ten roadmaps to joy. The roads are clearly marked. They are not all well paved. Some are full of potholes, some are gravel, some are steep and uphill, some are winding, and some are narrow. But they are all going in the right direction.

My friend, Linda, had neglected to use the roadmaps. She was looking for joy on the wrong roads. She felt no self-esteem because she had neglected to pay attention to eternal perspective, and thus, she felt no joy!

If we could part the veil, just you and me, for only a few minutes and be able to look into the past, what would we see? We would see the two of us as sisters, maybe even in long flowing white gowns, shouting for joy because we know we were coming to Earth. And if we could part the veil in the other direction, after this life, what would we see?

I know what you're thinking. You are saying to yourself, "Well, the future hasn't happened yet, so there's nothing to see." You and I must make the future happen now! First by hanging on to the vision of it, and second, by seeking eternal joy!

I invite you,
My sweet young sisters,
To visit with me
For awhile.
In these pages
Stay with me,
Linger yet awhile

And let me tell you
What I know about
Joy!

The kind of joy
That is worth
The price paid
And the thoughts spent,
The kind of joy
Worth the roads
Travelled.
It is not the
Kind of joy
You might be expecting.
It is joy that is pink,
Not red, like many
Might tell you
Joy should be.

What is that you ask?

"How can I possibly
Know about joy,
Being so young
In life?"

Because

Sweet Sister,
You will know
Sorrow, too.

"And your sorrow
Will be turned into
Joy!"

JOY OF PRAYER

"If thou art sorrowful, call on the Lord . . . that your souls may be joyful."

—D&C 136:29

There was no other place to start with Linda but at the beginning! "If you want joy, then you must seek it," I told her. And the first joy on the list is Prayer. Linda asked me why she should pray, how that would help her feel joy. I told her this true story:

There is a young lady who now lives in Idaho. Her high school years were a very hard time for her because she didn't date very much. In fact, she could count the dates she had on the fingers of one hand. When she graduated from high school and went on to college, she found that she still didn't date very much. As she grew into her middle twenties and then her late twenties, she watched her younger sisters, one by one, enter womanhood and marriage and start their families. She wondered why wasn't she as talented and pretty and popular as they and as some of her friends and associates were? Perhaps the Lord was holding these blessings from her because of something that she had done in her life. Perhaps He wasn't pleased with her. She wondered why life had passed her by. She now realized that it might be many years before she married and maybe she may never marry. She felt sad and lonely and had no self-esteem. Maybe she wasn't as good as everybody else.

She thought perhaps she should go on a mission, so she went to see the bishop. He interviewed her, found her worthy, and gave her the necessary papers to fill out. She went home to work on them. The following week as she was leaving to go turn in her paperwork, the thought struck her, "How can I motivate or

9

inspire anybody in the gospel of Jesus Christ? How can I teach them about Heavenly Father's love for them if I do not feel His love for me as a person? If I feel like I'm not worthy to do this, what makes me think that I can go out and motivate anyone when I have not found motivation and self-esteem in the gospel of Jesus Christ myself?" She decided to hold on to her papers and search out in her heart and in her mind all that she could to try to understand why she didn't feel good about herself and why she felt like she wasn't as good as others around her. She turned to the scriptures. She began to study them. She began to investigate. Soon she discovered that all she had been taught in Primary and M.I.A. and on into her young womanhood about Father loving us because we are His daughters was very acceptable to her. Logically, she could understand that He loved her, He was her father, and she was His daughter. But even though her mind could understand this, in her heart she didn't feel His love for her. She didn't feel the joy of His love for her. She didn't feel joy in going to Him and talking with Him. She realized that she didn't feel close to Him. She didn't feel any joy in being His daughter.

She read in the Doctrine and Covenants 136:29, "And if thou art sorrowful, call on the Lord thy God that thy soul may be joyful." She decided to put it to the test, and she began to pray. At first it was hard for her to pray, because she had not been used to doing it. She had not been used to addressing Father in anything more than a two or three minute salutation. She decided to work a little harder, and she began to study exactly *what* prayer was. She began to practice everyday having more tender, sincere, and powerful prayers—"Dear Father, I thank thee; Dear Father, please forgive me; Dear Father, these are the things that I desire; Father, please bless me; Father, this is what I intend to accomplish this day; Father, this is what I have accomplished this day; Father, bless me as to the things that I need to know; inspire me as to the paths I need to travel; Father, have patience with me."

Day after day and prayer after prayer, she made a sincere, honest effort, and nothing came. No sweet feeling of joy filled her heart, and her faith waivered. But she prayed harder and longer, not weaker or less. As the prayers moved into days, weeks, and then months, she decided that even though no sweet feeling of joy in knowing that Father loved her had come, she needed to serve this mission. She needed to pull away from those selfish thoughts that were turning inward and making her feel weak and go out and serve Him on a mission. So she decided to turn the paperwork in. Before going to the bishop that afternoon, she stopped off at her sister's home to share the news. Parking her car in the backyard, she walked up the back steps. As she opened the kitchen door, she heard the sweetest strains of a piano. Her sister was playing primary songs for her children. She paused there in the kitchen, listening, and suddenly the words of the song, "I Know My Heavenly Father Loves Me," came flooding into her mind and into her spirit, but more importantly into her heart. Starting at the very center of her heart, pricking it like a little needle, then pushing through and filling her whole soul from the crown of her head to the bottom of her feet. She felt, not heard, her Heavenly Father's love for her. For the first time in her life she saw herself as He sees her. She saw herself not as a weak and deprived young woman but as the daughter of the living God. She saw that she was loved and cherished and felt the clock stand still as God's love warmed her, inspired her, and healed her! She knew *who* she was! She had gained eternal perspective! So overcome was she with this sweetest, most incredible love that she fell to her knees. And there, in that kitchen, she expressed a prayer of gratitude and thanksgiving to Him for being her kind and loving and patient Father. She expressed a prayer of repentance for having counseled Him and not being patient with Him. And she expressed, above all, her love for Him. This young woman knew that communication and joy like that could never have come, except through tender yet very strong and powerful prayer.

I have had that same experience and so have many people. It is real and possible. May I share another story with you.

Another Latter-day Saint girl who had really lost her way came to visit me. She was doing things that made those who loved her feel great sorrow. She was living far from happiness and joy. She knew it because she was miserable.

She asked for help to get her life back in order, but when I outlined the things she should do, she became upset and rebellious. She looked over my list and crumpled it on the table.

"You can do those things on that list, Anita, and it will make you feel better, but not me. I'm not the type. I have done too many ugly things." She argued far into the night. It wasn't easy trying to convince her that even though we don't always have Heavenly Father's approval, He still loves us. She felt so awful about herself she was sure He could never love her.

Finally she agreed to start somewhere, and that somewhere was prayer.

Just like the girl from Idaho, it was not easy at first. She struggled very much because she felt so far away. She said that at first she was ashamed. She didn't know what to say, and then she would just cry. But little by little, week after week, month after month, she found a greater comfort and need to pray.

Then one day it happened. As she was ending her prayer one evening, she told Heavenly Father that she was truly sorry. She told Him that she knew He was her Father, and she told Heavenly Father that she loved Him. As she ended her prayer and got off her knees, she was overcome with the sweetest peace. Into her mind and heart came the words, "I love you, too, my daughter."

When she described her experience to me, she could hardly contain her joy, so great was her self-esteem!

And so, how do we pray? For us, as sisters, and especially as young women, I would like to share these thoughts with you:

1. When we get on our knees, we need to have a sweetness present in our hearts. Do not offer prayers of habit or routine. Try to talk to Him often with new words and about different thoughts each time.

2. We should think about Him in a loving way. He is not the stone-faced, harsh image that many picture Him to be. He is loving, like President Kimball, or your own earthly father, or any great and loving man you can relate to. His love for you is perfect. You don't always have His approval, but you always have His love.

   His love is patient. He is eager to hear you to inspire you, but He can't unless you come to Him. He wants to comfort you and heal wounds and soothe you with His divine love, but He can't unless you call upon Him. He is patiently and gently waiting.

3. We should be willing to obey and conform to His will. We should be careful to ask only for those things that are right and tell Him, "Father, thy will be done." He knows what we need in order to become more like Him, and we must have patience with Him and His purposes for us.

4. We should ask Him to help us see our weaknesses without being defeated by them. We should ask for help in gaining control, but not be overwhelmed because it takes time. Remember, once we gain control over an area, it takes a *lot* of practice to be in control 100 percent of the time! We need to be honest in our prayers of repentance and face Father with the truth. He will help us see our weaknesses and help us overcome them.

5. We must ask for and seek the Holy Ghost. If you are to feel joy, it will come by the power of the Holy Ghost, because love is a gift of the Spirit. Your prayers are answered by the power of the Holy Ghost.

6. We should pray for our family, our friends, our schoolwork, our talents, etc.

7. We should express our love to Father and for His son Jesus Christ, and for the gift of the Holy Ghost.

8. Include all else that is in our lives that we choose to discuss with Him.

9. We must not become discouraged if our prayers, at first, do not seem inspired or answered. We must all grow to that point; it is part of being proven.

Praying is a great experience if you take time to travel the right road. Prayer is the way to know Heavenly Father loves you. It is the way to feel His love for you and see yourself through His eyes. And when that happens, you begin to have eternal perspective and the joy of knowing who you really are.

He promised to give us the roadmaps, remember? He promised to mark them clearly:

If thou art sorrowful, call on the Lord . . . that your souls may be joyful. (Doctrine & Covenants 136:29.)

Not very long ago, maybe twelve, sixteen, or eighteen short years ago, you were talking with Father, probably often and everyday. You were experiencing that great joy of being in His presence. You can have that experience again as often as you would like. You can be in His presence every time you kneel in prayer. And every time you can know that if your prayers are sincere, He really is listening. He is listening because He cares. He loves you with all of His heart. You mean so much to Him. He is looking for you to visit with Him each day. Every time you kneel, you can know He is there and loves you. That, my friends, is indeed joy!

JOY OF OBEDIENCE

"I, the Lord . . . will crown the faithful with joy."

—D&C 52:43

As Linda began to soften her heart, build her faith in prayer, and trust her Father in Heaven, her love for Him began to increase, and she wanted to be more obedient. She was still objecting to so many rules, however, and saw obedience as a restraint on her life.

She felt that perhaps so many laws and commandments might be stopping her from experiencing part of life that would make her wiser or happier. I explained to her that that was one of Satan's greatest weapons. His slogan is:

> You only go around once in life so get all the action, money, gusto, sex, and whatever else you want, and get it all RIGHT NOW!

Heavenly Father knows this is wrong. If you break a law, you limit yourself. For example, how foolish not to obey the laws of gravity and jump off a building! If you obey or respect the law of gravity, you will wear a parachute. If everyone obeys the traffic laws, you feel safe while riding on the highway. But if everyone was to disregard them, you would not feel safe to drive, and your freedom would be limited. Laws are to help us gain control so that we can have freedoms. A lot of people don't understand this. They only see laws as restricting freedoms. Let me illustrate by sharing this story about one of my children.

When you turn fourteen in the Church, you are given a dance card which enables you to attend Stake dances. Now, when one of our children was about to turn fourteen, we sat down as a family and talked about the curfew hours for these Stake dances.

Unanimously we decided that 11:30 would be the curfew hour. Since the Stake dances ended at 11:00, that would leave thirty minutes to come home. He went to see the bishop, had his interview, and obtained his dance card. Then came the night of the first Stake dance. He walked into the kitchen, looking very handsome, and said, "Well, Mom, I'm ready to go to the dance. The guys will be here to pick me up in a little while, and I'll be home at 1:00." I looked at him blankly, "1:00? But our curfew was 11:30." "Yes, I know, Mother, but this is a special night; this is the first dance, and we want to go to the pizza parlor afterwards. By the time we get there it will be 11:30, and by the time we eat and leave it will be 12:30, so I'll be home about 1:00."

And I said, "No, son, the agreement was 11:30."

He argued, "But I don't want an 11:30 curfew this one time. Next time I'll come in at 11:30. But this time I want a 1:00 curfew."

"No, the agreement was 11:30. If we break the rules now, we'll have to do it again another time."

"No, you won't," he argued, "I'll be in at 1:00 tonight and 11:30 from here on."

"Well, son, that's not what we agreed upon. We agreed that you would exercise the 11:30 curfew."

And so the argument started back and forth, back and forth until finally he realized that I was not going to give in and that he indeed had to uphold the 11:30 curfew. But he did not want to give in and begrudgingly, accepting the 11:30 curfew, said, "All right, I'll come in at 11:30, but believe me, I can't wait till I'm an adult. I'll do anything I want. Adults don't have any rules."

To which I said, "But they do have rules, son; adults have lots of rules. Why, Dad and I live by rules."

"No, you don't, you can come in any time you want."

"That's true, but if we were to come in at 5:00 a.m. and have to be up by 7:00, we know how tired and exhausted we would be."

"Well, I don't believe it. I think you can do whatever you

want, and you don't have any rules to govern your life. Adults really don't have any."

And I said, "That's not true, the prisons are full of adults who have not learned to obey rules. They have not learned self-control. So society has had to take over and teach them responsibility. As you exercise responsibility and show control in your 11:30 curfew, next year we'll extend your curfew to 11:35!"

Well, not to be argumentative, but not wanting to lose the argument, he grudgingly said, "All right then, I can't wait until I'm the God of my own world, because then there will be no rules, and I'll have no rules to obey!"

Now at this point, his Dad, who was sitting at the kitchen table, raised his head and looked up and said, "Just a minute, son; now you're really wrong. You see, God is God because He obeys *all* the rules. And when you become perfect in your obedience to all the rules in life, then and only then will you be the God of your own world."

And so you see, obedience is not a restraint as Satan would have you believe. The whole point of life on this earth and in the next world is to become perfect so we can be Gods. To become perfect like God means to follow the recipe, or steps, or, as He put it, the laws.

Do you want to have freedom? The key to freedom is obedience. If we don't want the roads to be too dangerous to drive on, we had all better obey the traffic laws.

We are free to choose. Heavenly Father knows what will make us free.

President Kimball once said that God is good. He is eager to forgive. He wants us to perfect ourselves and maintain control of ourselves. He doesn't want Satan or others to control our lives. We must learn that keeping our Heavenly Father's commandments presents the *only* path to total control of ourselves.

When I disobey a law, whether it is a law of the land or a law of God, I feel no joy. But when I am obedient, I feel a great satisfaction and joy in knowing I am developing self-control.

I used to weigh 140 pounds. That is forty pounds overweight for my small-boned five-foot frame. I disobeyed the laws of good eating habits and was out of control. But as soon as I learned to obey those laws, I lost the weight, was in control, and felt joy again! Self-control comes through obedience.

If you want self-control and feel like it slips by you too many times, let me share some ideas that helped me to hold on to self-control.

A. ORGANIZE YOURSELF

I am amazed at how many people wake up every morning and whatever falls in their lap is what life is all about. And they live like this day after day, year after year, letting life dictate to them.

Get up! Rise up! Set goals! Make plans! Schedule priorities! Do something now!

Set Priorities

Make a set plan for your life by the day, the month, the year. First, make an overall priority list. May I suggest one?

1. Seek first the kingdom of God with all our heart (emotion and feeling), might (self-control), mind (intellect and thought), and strength (time and energy).

2. Have goals: daily, lifetime, and eternal goals.

3. Seek the companionship and direction of the Holy Ghost by praying for it and living worthy to receive it.

4. Take care of your physical body by proper diet and exercise so that you can feel good and be prepared to handle your responsibilities.

5. Love, honor, and respect your parents.

6. Strengthen your extended families, parents, brothers, and sisters, etc. Love them, elevate them, and add your testimonies to their lives.

7. Magnify your church callings and be willing to serve the Lord.

8. Serve your fellowman in any way you possibly can.

9. Develop your talents and intellectual capacity in order to serve the Lord more and increase your potential.

10. Prepare to be a wife and a mother in Zion.

How can this priority list be used everyday?

Daily

1. Seek the Kingdom of God—
   Read the scriptures each day.
   Pray morning and evening.

2. Set goals—
   Write down each morning what you need to accomplish for the day in order of importance; cross them off as you finish. If you don't finish, add them to the next day.

3. Seek the Spirit—
   You've already asked for it in your prayers, now take time throughout the day to pay attention to the Spirit.

4. Take care of your physical body—
   Exercise, even ten minutes each day.
   Eat properly.

5. Love your parents—
   Do something each day to serve or honor your parents.

6. Strengthen your family—
   On a daily basis, include them in your prayers.

7. Magnify your church calling—
   Take a few minutes each day to ponder what you can do to improve your efforts.

8. Serve others—
   Be ready to help; pay attention to opportunities that may come your way.

9. Develop your potential—
   Find time each day, even if only ten minutes, to refuel and fill your spirit. Read a good book, talk to a friend, work on a hobby.

10. Prepare for Motherhood—
    Be clean and chaste.
    Date boys that will honor you and have the potential to take you to the temple.

How can this be used every month?

Monthly

1. Seek the Kingdom of God—
   Attend all your meetings.
   Keep the Sabbath day holy.
   Keep the commandments.

2. Set goals—
   The first of every month write down what you need to accomplish for that month in order of importance.

3. Seek the Spirit—
   Fast on Fast Sunday.

4. Take care of your physical body—
   Lose weight if necessary; exercise and eat properly.

5. Love your parents—
   Concentrate on building and developing this relationship.
   Go on outings; have projects together, talk to them.

6. Strengthen your family—
   Hold family get-togethers.
   Express your love.

7. Magnify church callings—
   Be dependable.

8. Serve others—
   Minister to the sick and needy.
   Be a missionary.

9. Develop your potential—
   Take a class or begin a new hobby or continue to be educated in your specified areas of interest by reading and practicing.

10. Prepare for Motherhood—
    Learn homemaking skills.
    Be modest in your dress.

How can this be used over a lifetime?

Lifetime

1. Seek the Kingdom of God—
   Stick to your commitments and covenants.
   Obey the Prophet (acquire food storage, plant a garden, keep a journal, do genealogy, etc.)

2. Set goals—
   Each January write down your goals for the year and for your life; reevaluate year to year.

3. Seek the Spirit—
   Obey the Spirit and try to be teachable so that you

can continue growing.

4. Take care of your physical body—
   Have regular yearly checkups.

5. Love your parents—
   Demonstrate in word and deed your love.

6. Strengthen your family—
   Do genealogy.
   Support them in all their righteous endeavors (attend reunions, missionary farewells, blessings, etc.) where possible.

7. Magnify church callings—
   Never feel you have done enough. You should accept callings until you die.

8. Serve others—
   Continue to be a missionary.
   Pay your fast offerings and support the missionary fund.

9. Develop your potential—
   Spend time to further the world around you. Get an education.
   Travel, take classes, be curious, read.
   Take time for yourself.

10. Motherhood—
    Marry in the temple.
    Learn all you can from parenting classes.
    Seek inspiration from Heaven.

B. SET GOALS

To establish and achieve goals you must:

1. **"Seek Ye First The Kingdom Of God"** (Matthew 6:33).
   Make sure your goal is a righteous one. Would

the Lord approve? If your intentions are pure, you will have inspiration in selecting proper goals in your life. Always refer to your priorities list when selecting worthy goals.

2. Be Specific

Set clearly in your mind EXACTLY what it is you want to accomplish and HOW you are going to do it. Your goal must be specific, and you must picture how you are going to accomplish it. A good way to plan is by asking yourself:

What am I going to do?
When am I going to do it?
How am I going to do it?
Who could help me?
Where can I do it?
How long do I need?
Why am I going to do this?

3. Write It Down

There is a real strength in writing down goals. When you ponder goals, ideas come. As quickly as one comes, it can leave you or become confused as other thoughts appear. Keep a separate notebook or journal, even just for goals and ideas. Refer to it often. If necessary, repeat your goals aloud during the day.

I have a friend who has written down the goal for her eternal life. A little piece of paper taped inside a kitchen cupboard says, "I am going *home.*" She repeats that aloud at breakfast, lunch, and dinner. She'll make it to the Celestial Kingdom; it is her goal. Keeping it constantly forward in her daily thoughts helps her live more earnestly each day. She has eternal perspective.

President Kimball said that we must have goals to make progress, encouraged by keeping records.

Progress is easier when it is timed, checked, and measured. Goals are good. Laboring with distant aim sets the mind in a higher key and puts us at our best. Goals should always be made to a point that will make us reach and strain.

4. Report Your Goals

Go to that journal and notebook and record your progress. You should also include the Lord (even a friend or parent) in your goals. You should ask the Lord for His approval and also report your progress.

Tell Him of your desires and commitments. Don't you think He is interested?

Reporting goals out loud is motivating because it makes the goal more of a commitment. It keeps the clutter off the road and helps us see how far we've come.

5. Set Realistic Goals

There are short-range goals and long-range goals. They tie in with your DAILY, MONTHLY, and LIFETIME priorities. A short-range goal would be: take piano lessons and practice one hour a day. A long-range goal would be: give a recital and teach others.

Having a few repeated successes will help you gain confidence in tackling more difficult ones. All goals should make us reach; some should make us strain. Don't set goals, however, that are improbable. If I set a goal to be an Olympic swimmer right now, it is highly improbable for me to make it. My age, for one thing, would stop me, but my other priorities wouldn't allow the time necessary. If you set an improbable goal or improbable time limit, and you don't meet that goal, your confidence will weaken, and you will have not benefitted from that goal. Start with simple ones and add the more difficult ones later.

6. Commit To Them

President Kimball's now famous motto declares "DO IT!" What good is any plan, no matter how strong the desire to succeed, if ACTION doesn't take place.

I once hired a floral designer because she marched into my office and presented her goals to me with an enthusiasm that left me sparkling. She told me what she could do for my company and why. She listed her goals for herself and our firm. I was so impressed! Within one week I knew it was all "go and no-show." Talk is cheap. (In the design business we are supposed to say "Inexpensive"!) That enthusiasm was there, and she talked and talked. But I didn't see any action. I gave her the benefit of the doubt. At the end of four weeks, the enthusiasm had paled, nothing was accomplished, and she was dismissed. *Goals without action equal nothing.*

"Help us, oh God, to remember that little things completed are better than big things planned." (Peter Marshall.)

7. The Next Level

A goal should be the next level and not the final result! Most people become frustrated when they plan for a goal, then upon reaching it, they level off. If temple marriage is your goal, and you reach it, then other goals need to be established quickly to make the marriage a success. Always plan your goals with the next level in mind.

C. PRAYER AND FASTING

Prayer and fasting are two of the great basics of self-control. We should fast to draw closer to the Spirit. Even though we've already discussed prayer, it needs to be re-emphasized that prayer adds great power to self-control. The mistake many people make is that they pray and then let the Lord "do it for them."

A young teenager suffering from a smoking habit thought if she prayed the Lord would stop her. It was *her* body that was in control of *her* spirit, and Father would not take control. It is up to us to learn that our spirits must be in control of our bodies. But through prayer and fasting we can gain the inspiration we need to encourage us and help *ourselves* gain that control.

D. SCRIPTURES

You've heard it over and over—read your scriptures.

"It's no longer a question of whether you have been through the standard works, but whether the life and light in them has somehow passed through the very skin of your bodies and enlivened you." (Madsen, *Highest in Us*, page 26, Bookcraft.)

Are you reading the scriptures daily? If not, you are missing personal words with God everyday. There is something eternal in those words. We have heard them before. They are familiar to us. As we read them, the veil thins, and we can sense where home really is. When we get that close to home, we get closer to a glimpse of how great we really were before we came here! That feeling of greatness can linger all day.

In studying the scriptures, you can know the nature of God. You can read His mind. It's great! You can begin to see the great plan for yourself—you begin to increase your faith in yourself. You begin to have eternal perspective!

E. ATTEND CHURCH

How can you keep your faith strong and be diligent in *receiving* the Spirit if you don't attend your meetings and pay attention to the Spirit? How can you go to Father in prayer without having sung songs of praise to Him or paid devotions to Him and His Son? How can you try to discover your potential and make plans for gaining the Celestial Kingdom unless you renew your baptismal covenants with the sacrament?

As my friend Linda gained control over those aspects of her life, she made a wonderful discovery. Many other avenues of control became easier for her. For example, as she learned to organize herself, she found she had more time to practice the piano. Through this she discovered that she had a great talent lying dormant, and the required practice brought it forth. This recognition of her talents turned to new levels of self-confidence and self-esteem.

As she developed in fasting and prayer, she found a closeness with Father, and her love for Him heightened. She *desired* to obey His commandments. This brought her an inner strength and peace.

As she read the scriptures, she became aware of the personality of God and knew He loved her with a perfect love. She knew she *always* had His love. This knowledge restored her personal self-worth.

And as she attended church diligently, she found opportunities to make friends, share her newly-discovered talent, accept assignments, and be with people who had the same goals in life. She truly was learning that obedience brings self-esteem, and self-esteem brings joy.

But Linda did not learn this overnight; she worked slowly, but diligently. Like the young man who became interested in the Church because of his friends who invited him to play on the Teachers' basketball team. After many months he became interested in the gospel, took the missionary lessons, became convinced that the Church was true, and asked to be baptized.

At his baptismal interview, the bishop said to him, "Well, I find you to be a fine young man, I find you to be worthy of baptism, and I'm going to recommend you for baptism; however, are you aware of your problem with profanity?"

The young man, who definitely had a problem with profanity, was not aware of it and answered, "Well, Hell, bishop, what do you mean?"

And the bishop said, "Son, you have a problem with profanity, and I would like to talk to you about it. That kind of language is not conducive to a young man who will hold the Holy Priesthood of God. What would be your plan?"

As they talked for the next little while in the bishop's office, this young man decided that he would simply quit. The bishop, who was realistic, said, "Well, that will take time, you know, to learn control over something like that. It takes time to develop self-control. Why don't you set yourself a realistic goal?"

And so the young man set himself a goal for one year. He decided that during the next twelve months he would eliminate one profane word a month from his vocabulary. The first month he would allow himself only twelve swear words. The second month he would only say eleven swear words, ten the next month, nine the next, and so on, until in one year's time he would have realized his goal of using no profanity.

He was baptized, and that first month he did very well the first week. But the second week he used all twelve swear words. He really had to struggle the last two weeks, biting his tongue, grinding his teeth, struggling and sputtering, but he made it. He made it. At the end of the month, he had said only twelve swear words! The next month came, and he struggled through that first week, and the second week he slipped and said a few. The third week he slipped and said a few more, and by the end of the last week he had said his whole alotment of eleven swear words. The next month came with its alotment of ten. He struggled and fought and watched carefully every word he said, but by the end of the month he had said only ten swear words. Now the fourth month came which was July, and this time he found that during the early weeks of the month he was just doing fine, a word here, a word there. Carefully counting, by the end of July he only said nine swear words. Then came August. Something happened, disappointment, frustration, and all that hard work, and all that effort was wiped out in a few paragraphs when he said many more than just a dozen swear words.

Now he could have given up, thinking "Oh, well, what's the use, I'm not in control; I'll never gain control. I've worked hard for four months and did just fine, but you see I'm not really worth it. I'm not made of the stuff that Gods are made of. I can't really do it. I'm not good enough."

He could have. He could have stopped right there like so many of us have. When we try and struggle for control and obedience, and we do just fine, we feel joy. But when we slip and fall back and then quit, we think we can't go on. This would have been his case had he let himself listen to Satan, but he didn't. In August he felt defeated. But in September he gathered his courage, he gathered his strength, and in September, he said only four! He went farther than what he even thought he could. He mustered new strength and commitment. And long before his intended goal of one year was over he had conquered his profanity problem completely.

We must remember that once we do gain control, it takes a lot of practice to be in control 100 percent of the time, perhaps a lifetime of practice and on into eternity. Being faithful and obedient is an uphill road. But oh the joy each time we overcome an August in our lives! "I the Lord will crown the faithful with joy!" (D&C 52:43.)

JOY OF WORK

"... ye have joy in the fruit of your labors."

—D&C 6:31

The Lord intended us to work hard because He works hard. Elder Neal A. Maxwell has written:

> God's work is unimaginably difficult work. It is very real, very relentless and repetitive. His course is one eternal round, He has said. But His work is also His glory. And we, His children everywhere, are His work. We are at the center of His purposes and concerns. "We are the people of his pasture, and the sheep of his hand." (*Even As I Am*, Deseret Book, 1982.)

Our Father knows what dark thoughts can be planted in idle minds and what ungodlike acts can be committed with idle hands. Part of Linda's problem was feeling sorry for herself. She shut herself away from others so as not to feel the pain of the "lack of's" in her life and so found herself with an idle mind and idle hands. A perfect bed of rotting soil in which Satan could not only plant, but even cultivate his giant roots of weakness.

My father grew up in the worst slums in Houston, Texas. A perfect place for idle hands and minds. He was a poor Mexican slum boy. Often he went to school without any shoes because his family couldn't afford them. They didn't have running water, plumbing, or electricity in their home at all. He used to tell us stories of when the Bijou would overflow, and he and his brothers and sisters would have to swim downriver and retrieve the outhouses that had floated away. They lived in an area where the Mexican people were looked down upon and degraded and segregated from the rest of the community. Often they didn't have enough to eat and always maintained a diet of starchy foods, beans, and tortillas. They never had a car. They never had any household appliances. They never took family vacations. They were slum poor. But they were a happy family because in that home they learned the joy of hard work. In their family it was required that they speak two languages: their native English and their cultural Spanish tongues. It was required that they maintain good grades in school and to be the best that they could be. It was required that they get a part-time job and contribute money to the whole family. It was required to do the chores and share in the family responsibilities.

My father never complained. He said that no one in that family ever complained. They knew the joy of hard work. Many of their Mexican neighbors would say, "Why do you work so hard? Why do you care? We're poor; we live in the slums; we're Mexicans. This is all that life will ever do for us." And those neighbors took it easy; they didn't work as hard. They didn't try as hard, and they didn't learn as much.

Often my father had no shoes. In the middle of winter one year when he was about eight, his shoes gave out. He had patched and roped them together for the last time. It was a bitterly cold school day, and his mother told him not to walk the five miles each way. Saturday would bring him another pair of shoes, she hoped. He said that he had to go. At school he was learning great things; at school he could work and make things happen. So he started his walk in the freezing cold.

Along the way he met his friend, Tomas. Tomas asked him why he would go to school with no shoes in that weather. My father told him that his feet ached but that his heart ached more.

I know that little children are filled with more pure love than we can ever imagine, and I know that my father inspired Tomas with his diligence and his determination to work hard because Tomas said, "Alex, you carry my books, and I'll carry you." And so he did—one little burden on another's back—five miles each way.

I have no idea where Tomas is or who he is, but he inspired

me. I am so grateful that he helped my father keep his commitment to himself. Keeping those commitments and learning hard work helped shape a slum child's life. I am so grateful for all the times that my father has carried me on his back; he has done it with the pure love of Christ.

Those children in my father's family could have sat back and said, "We don't need to go to school. We don't need to work hard. We don't need to try. We're poor; we're Mexican. We're a minority, and that's all life will ever bring us." But their mother inspired them to do more. She taught her children hard work, self-reliance, and that they must be the best that they can be. To try with all of their might to do their level best. She taught them by her own example, never complaining, never seeing the mud, only the stars, always being positive. She taught them by working hard herself.

My father was a straight A student in high school. In his junior year his math teacher gave him a B, the only one he has ever received. He went home with a heavy heart. He told his mother he knew he deserved an A. His work had been almost perfect. She told him to go back to the teacher and seek an explanation. And he did. He approached his teacher with sincere bewilderment at receiving a B. You can imagine how it crushed his spirit as he felt the teacher's pure disgust when he replied, "Yes, your work was correct, but I'll never give a Mexican an A."

My father could have returned to a home of mediocrity and complacency. "Well, son, that's okay. A B is good enough. That's okay, son, this is what you expect. We're Mexicans, and you're lucky to get a B." But he didn't. He returned to a home of excellence, of hard work, and motivation. My little grandmother spiritually put her arms around her son's bruised self-esteem and taught him how great it was to be a Mexican! She taught him to change his thinking and to replace his doubt with hard work and thoughts of "I can, and I will." That experience could have been devastating, but instead it was turned into one that inspired him!

Out of her seven slum children came an army officer, a

pharmacist-businessman, a chemical engineer, a scientist, a real estate tycoon, an artist-educator, and a doctor. Two are millionaires, and the others are very comfortable financially. Seven slum children and seven successes. Why? Because they learned at a very young age what the joy of hard work really is. Their magnificent mother taught them.

Satan would try to deceive you that having to work hard means being picked on. He would like you to believe a "life on easy street" is better. These are lies. And if you are listening to those lies, you had better pay attention to the truth. Before you know it, you can be caught up in the day of idleness. If it hardens around you, it will be extremely difficult to break away from it. You will find yourself calloused in slothfulness and apathy!

Laziness leads to a lot of ugly behaviors. It leads to attitudes like

> "I don't care."
> "Something for nothing."
> "Average will do."
> "This is good enough."

and so on.

The Kingdom of God will be composed of hard workers. Satan knows this and is teaching the world that mediocrity is acceptable. Generations are being taught that mediocrity is all that is accepted. That it is okay to whitewash the fence instead of sanding, priming and painting it.

Once my husband and I rated each other for fun. We were discussing our levels of achievement, mostly spiritual. We were rating each one in accordance with his or her potential. We decided that I was about 85 percent. Feeling fairly secure and smug about that, I was confident that 85 percent was well within acceptance. About an later—with, as Joseph Smith put it, pure intelligence flowing through me—came the thought and message that "85 percent is working, Anita, but it's only the last 10-15 percent that counts to the Lord!"

There are reasons the Lord asks you to work hard. Partly because He works hard. Also because He knows busy minds and hands have little use for Satan's temptations. And because if we don't work hard, we cannot truly know joy!

He commanded us to "be ye therefore perfect even as your Father which is in Heaven is perfect." That seems like a heavy load to place on our shoulders. But He knows that if He said "Be perfect in *just one area* that your Father in Heaven is perfect in" we probably wouldn't work hard even in that one area.

Expect perfection from yourself and those around you. Not expecting harshness or anxiety, but expecting love and accomplishment. You can become perfect in specific areas in your life: a talent, a gospel principle, a personality trait, etc. But realize that you will not reach perfection in the total sense of the word in mortality. Total perfection is not necessary now. *Striving* for it, *working hard* toward it is.

When I decided to take flying lessons, I wanted the best instructor there was. Rumors of instructors who "cranked" out pilots made me determined to find an excellent instructor. As I asked around, one name kept appearing. After meeting the man and determining that he was indeed a qualified instructor, I began my training. Difficult was not an adequate word for the course of instruction he put me through. If the FAA required you to fly within 300 feet of a target, he required you to do it within 50 feet. If the FAA required five hours under the instrument hood, he required ten. If the FAA required you to recover from a stall, he required recovery from a nose dive. He was demanding. The day of the check-ride came. Nervous does not even begin to describe my state that day! I could not sleep the night before; there were butterflies in my stomach, and my hands trembled. The written test went by too quickly, and the FAA examiner and I climbed into the airplane.

I was amazed at how easy and simple the whole exam was; nothing compared to what my instructor had put me through. As the examiner was signing me off, he said, "If you could have a rating of perfect, I'd give it to you. Of all the students I have passed, your instructor's are the best. Nearly, if not perfect." After the noise and hilarity were over, and I had a quiet moment with my instructor, I told him what the examiner had said. I asked, "Why do your students do so much better?" "Because," he answered, "I expect them to be perfect."

He learned the secret, and it paid off for him. If he'd expected anything less, that's exactly what the students would have given him. Had he been mediocre, as a lot of instructors are, his students would have been mediocre. *When you are learning, you understand and know only the levels you are taught.* If he had said the FAA requires you to fly 300 feet on this mark, his students would have done just that, perhaps not even realizing they could do better.

The Lord does nothing in mediocrity, and He expects us to be like Him, looking for excellence and working hard for it. He has promised that joy will be the reward.

"... and ye shall have joy in the fruits of your labors."

Most of us have had experiences where we just did "enough to get by" whether in school, on a project, hobby, at home, whatever. When it was finished, and we got a "satisfactory" grade or attention, we felt just okay. There wasn't a feeling of great excitement; somehow we wanted to pass over the whole thing. Now compare that to the homework, exam, project, hobby, whatever that we slaved over. After lots of hard work, we received the grade or attention we wanted. Deep in our souls we know that we earned it. That feeling is what I'm talking about. JOY! Joy in the fruits of your *labors!*

If you haven't had an experience like that, if you've been "getting by," now is a good time to try. Go ahead, test it. Find something weak in your life and dig in! Work hard! Get on the right road.

It's not important that you are better than anybody else. It is only important that you are the best YOU can be.

Joy of Work

If you can't be a pine on top of the hill,
Be a scrub in the valley—but be
The best little scrub by the side of the rill
Be a bush, if you can't be a tree.

If you can't be a bush, be a bit of the grass
And some highway happier make.
If you can't be a mushie, then just be a bass
But the liveliest bass in the lake!

We can't all be captains, we've got to be crew
There's something for all of us here.
There's big work to do, and there's lesser to do
And the task we must do is the near.

If you can't be a highway, then just be a trail
If you can't be the sun, be a star.
It isn't by size that you win or you fail
But—being the best of whatever you are!

—Douglas Mallock

JOY OF EDUCATION

"If thou shalt ask, thou shalt receive revelation upon revelation, knowledge upon knowledge, that thou mayest know the mysteries and peaceable things—that which bringeth joy."

—D&C 42:61

It is a great promise that we can know those things which will bring us peace and joy. Close on the heels of this scripture is "but if ye are prepared ye shall not fear." (D&C 38:30.)

My friend, Linda, learned that she was afraid to experience life because of her past trials and struggles and disappointments. She told me that she had not been prepared for them. Every new trial brought more fear of failure. Fear absolutely wipes out any joy!

What we really fear in life is failure. The more education we have, the more we know about life, others, and ourselves. Thus, the better prepared we become for failures and disappointments. They aren't bad. They are learning experiences. They are bound to come, but they don't have to weaken us. These can be experiences to inspire us. But we must be prepared.

There are three areas of education I would like to discuss. They are spiritual, emotional, and academic education. Each is a part of the whole picture. Each is part of your eternal perspective. And each will bring you great joy!

SPIRITUAL

Becoming educated in life and salvation and all their purposes, including your own purpose on earth, is spiritual education.

"What is my purpose in life? What should I plan for? What do I do with my life?" These are questions in the minds of everybody.

It is important to view yourself through your Father in Heaven's eyes. The best way to do this is to read your patriarchal blessing often. If you do not have one, I encourage you to seek one. The patriarchal blessing is a gift from God and can help answer many questions of your future.

Linda had not read her patriarchal blessing in years. She found it, dusted it off, and through a simple exercise discovered a part of herself she had missed.

At the top of the page I had her write:

MY PATRIARCHAL BLESSING

LINEAGE

Here she wrote all her blessings and promises regarding her lineage. She was from Ephraim, the son of Joseph. Then she made four columns and titled them:

Council	Warnings	Gifts	Promises

She took her blessing apart line by line, sentence by sentence, and placed each line under the appropriate heading.

She discovered gifts she didn't know she had and some council she had been ignoring. She was inspired by the special promises if she would remain faithful. She began to see herself through her Heavenly Father's eyes.

> If the veil could be parted and you could see yourselves as you were when the Lord stood in the midst of the spirits, the noble and great ones, you would hear him say, 'These I will make my rulers,' . . . If the veil could be parted you could see who you were then, then have a recollection and vision of what awaits you—what the Lord had in mind for you noble and great ones who have come forth in this day and time—I do not think any of you would want to wile away your time. You would want to make sure that you are using those gifts and talents that God has endowed you with for the honor and glory of His name and the blessing of His children.
>
> —LeGrand Richards (*Ensign*)

Elder LeGrand Richards also shared these thoughts about his patriarchal blessing:

> I received a patriarchal blessing when I was only eight years old. Among other things it said, 'Thou hast not come here upon earth by chance, but in fulfillment of the decrees of the Almighty to accomplish a great work.' Then it went on in detail about what I would do. All my life as a boy, I prayed that if I did not come here by chance, that the Lord would help me to live so that I would not be deprived of the privilege of doing the work that he sent me to do. I cannot imagine anything that would be more disappointing than to return after this life and have the Lord say, 'Well, LeGrand, this is what we sent you to do, but you just wouldn't do it. You went off on a *detour*, and we had to raise up someone else to do your work for you.' (*Ensign*.)

His blessing was a guide and inspiration for him. It was a roadmap. He heeded its council and became one of the most beloved apostles of the Lord.

Linda wept as she read from her blessing, "Your Father in Heaven loves you." As she read of the choice gifts she'd been given and the work Father expects of her, she could see that He trusted her. She realized if she was of such great value to Him, she *must* be of value to herself also.

The gifts given to us in the preexistence are special, and unless we use them, they will be taken away. We must discover them, develop them, and then use them for the right purposes. The right purposes are the building of God's work and discovering our own mission here upon this earth.

Spiritual education means to cultivate our minds like we would a garden. We have to get the soil ready, fertilize it, rake it, groom it. Then the seeds can be planted. But that is not all; we have to water it and pull out weeds.

So you must get the spirit ready by finding out who you are; nourish it by reading the scriptures, going to church, praying, etc. Rake it by trying to get rid of bad habits or friends; and groom it by listening to the Holy Ghost. Then the Lord can plant seeds of understanding and knowledge. He can teach you about the "mysteries and peaceable things." He can teach you about His words. But that is not all. You must water the seeds by obeying the commandments and pull the weeds that Satan will try to ensnare you with.

You must do this on your own. Too many young people want to leave spiritual matters to their parents or church leaders. This won't work because the time is coming when no one will be able to make it on "borrowed" spirituality. A lot of people will try, but each person will have to be guided by the Spirit individually. Those who can't discern the Spirit may not make it!

You've been told, you are being warned now. FIND OUT WHO YOU ARE! Your patriarchal blessing is a good place to start. But don't stop there.

Read your scriptures. Pay attention to your spiritual leaders. Those are your parents, your teachers, and Priesthood leaders. Look for good people and copy their good habits.

Draw closer to Heavenly Father through prayer. Read your patriarchal blessing often. Challenge and stretch yourself to grow spiritually. The seeds will be planted, and one day not too distant, you'll begin to see the harvest.

EMOTIONAL

Emotional education is understanding and gaining knowledge about YOU. *Why do we have differences?*

Let's begin with a simple exercise. How would you describe a person without giving any reference to that person's talents, knowledge, looks, or accomplishments? Stop here and consider someone you know; think carefully about that statement and then describe the person.

This would have been impossible unless you knew that individual personally. You could not accurately describe somebody unless you were well acquainted with that person. How many times have you misjudged someone's character or personality simply by looking only at their outward appearances? After spending time getting acquainted with them, don't you often discover they are quite different from your first impression?

Let me describe a friend of mine.

She has a wonderful sense of humor which puts any person immediately at ease. This friend looks you straight in the eye. There is a genuine concern there for others' needs. She demonstrates compassion and care, is thoughtful, considerate, and takes great effort in discovering what special gifts she can offer to others. This wonderful woman is unselfish and would give you whatever she had that she thought you might need. She cares for her ailing mother and encourages her constantly. My friend has a serious illness that causes her great pain, yet she never complains. She is happy, friendly, and has great courage and common sense.

Now you have no idea what she looks like, what her knowledge is, what talents she may have, or whether or not she has accomplished much in her life. But you already know her. This description has influenced you to think of her in a positive way. It makes no difference that she is a tiny, five-foot blonde, slightly overweight, has a high school education, is an accomplished equestrian, plays the piano, is an entrepreneur in real estate, has a husband and three sons, and is not a member of the Church. Would your opinion of her be different had you only known the "physical facts" about her first?

We have not seen the Savior and yet when we describe Him, we describe qualities. The more qualities we discover about Him, the better we have come to know Him.

Describe yourself without any reference to your talents, knowledge, looks, or accomplishments. This will be impossible unless you really know yourself, unless you are honest with yourself, and have spent time in getting acquainted with YOU.

This is an important step to healthy self-esteem. You must be honest enough with yourself to describe who you are without any reference to your looks, talents, knowledge or accomplishments. You must be honest enough to acknowledge your qualities and strengths, as well as your weaknesses in character. You must be willing to study and search out WHO YOU ARE. It does require study. It also takes a great deal of courage to admit what you like and don't like about yourself.

But that isn't easy to do. It's a lot easier to blame others for your problems or weaknesses. The following are some common examples:

1. **Blaming family or environment.** "It's my family's fault." "I came from the wrong side of the tracks." "What do you expect from me? Look at my family." "People reject me because I'm poor."

2. **Blaming events.** "I only have bad luck." "Sure, she's a success, she's lucky." "The weather prevented me from doing it."

3. **Labeling.** "I am a lonely person." "I am a depressed person." I had a roommate in college that started every morning with the statement, "Oh, I am so depressed." She made me depressed. Whether we label ourselves or accept someone else's label of us, we are using a crutch.

4. **Blaming others.** "He hurt me." "The bishop fouled it up." "She insulted me, so I quit."

5. **Excusing our behavior.** "I was born this way." "This is inherited. My mom is just like this." "Well, everybody else does it." "Satan made me do it." "I am not organized." "I was sick."

Linda found that this was true with her. Remember some of the things she said (see first page). She blamed others and found fault with everything but herself.

Once she decided that she was special and unique, she decided she had differences for a reason. If everyone were the same, what would we learn from each other? Who would meet our needs since they would all be the same needs? Who would inspire us? Who would we be able to serve or inspire? What would be the use of interacting with each other? Nothing!

We were born with differences and individual uniqueness to be able to bless each other's lives. Sister Camilla Kimball put it this way:

> . . . the Lord does not judge us by what we have but by what we do with what we have. The rich may be haughty, the poor envious, the powerful cruel, the weak sniveling. And those between the extremes may well be complacent and lukewarm.
> To be rich is good, if you can be humble.
> To be learned is good, if you can be wise.
> To be healthy is good, if you can be useful.
> To be beautiful is good, if you can be gracious.
> There is, however, nothing inherently bad in being poor, unlettered, sickly, or plain.
> To be poor is good, if you can still be generous of Spirit.
> To be unschooled is good, if it motivates you to be curious.
> To be sickly is good, if it helps you to have compassion.
> To be plain is good, if it saves you from vanity.
> (Camilla Kimball, "Ye Are Free To Choose," pamphlet, page 18.)

I can go down both lists and write in the names of people who are rich, but humble; learned, but wise; healthy and always working for others; beautiful, but helping those around them to be beautiful, too; poor, but generous of spirit, always giving all they have; unschooled, but always learning something; sickly, but understanding of others and an example of courage; and plain, but confident and without guile.

As you ponder those statements, make your own list of those who fit these descriptions. It may surprise you to see those who are true successes. In the eyes of the world they may not be but to the Lord and themselves they are! And something else will surprise you, too. You will see how your life is blessed by their differences!

ACADEMIC

Increasing your understanding in a certain area of interest is your academic education.

It is important for us to be as educated a people as we possibly can. Do not be taken in by the old philosophy that a young woman will grow up, have babies, hang lace curtains, and bake bread the rest of her life.

First, every young woman needs to have some sort of education, if not for her livelihood, for the expansion of her Spirit! And second, life is so uncertain. Some will never marry in this life, some will lose husbands early through death or divorce, and some may need to supplement a husband's income because of the world's economic situation. Perilous times lay ahead. One thing is certain, nothing will be stable! Do not be duped into thinking you will be different. Never lose sight of the scripture, "If you are prepared, ye shall not fear." (D&C 38:30.)

Even a little education is better than none at all. Sister Kimball, speaking at the dedication of the chair in her honor at the college of Family Living at BYU, said:

> I would hope that every girl and woman would have the desire and ambition to qualify in two vocations: that of homemaking and that of preparing to make a living outside the home if and when the

occasion requires it.

Any woman may be under the necessity of earning her own living and helping to support dependent children. If she has been trained for the duties and emergencies of life which may come to her, she will be happier and have a greater sense of security.

It is sometimes urged that education for women is not as important as education for men, but there is no real difference. What we must be concerned with is preparation for life, and that preparation is continuing education.

Whether it is to make a living or rear children, men and women both need to have the knowledge that enhances their natural talents.

Living in this world has proven to be a voyage of continual discovery. I'm reluctant to have it end—I'm having too good a time.

It is important that our minds are expanded that we may be more in charge of our abilities. For example, if two people want to learn to paint and one buys a paint-by-number set and the other takes art lessons, which one will learn more completely? Which one will develop their ability to capture on canvas what they see? Which one will learn to combine and experiment with colors? Which one will have a future opportunity to teach others, perhaps even earn money?

The paint-by-number set gets you what you want right at the moment, but it is education that keeps you growing and gaining more forever.

Our minds were made to hold much knowledge. Scientists and psychologists have determined that we use only two percent to eight percent of our brains. Can you believe that! Ninety-two percent to 98 percent of our brains are unused! That means that there is more knowledge Father would have us gain. He uses 100 percent of His brain, and that's one reason He can gather the heavens, create worlds, and know the past and future.

What a waste of a good mind to let yourself slip into complacency. Getting an education can mean many things. For some it will be a formal college degree. For others it will be learning skills in typing, art, computers, etc. Along with all of these is the education of homemaking skills. Remember, we must:

1. Be prepared to meet life's emergencies and unexpected crisis with confidence.

2. Expand our minds and exercise our gifts, turning them into talents and being able to help others.

3. Gain joy from using our potential and realize we are growing.

Get out your patriarchal blessing and read it at least once a week. If you don't have one, see about getting one. Pay attention to the gifts mentioned. Write them down, seek after them. Search the scriptures for the meaning of our existence, not only here, but through all eternity.

As you do these things, you will begin to discover who you are. You will see the woman you were before you came here. Your spiritual knowledge will grow and blossom.

Through the knowledge that you are the daughter of the living God, you will begin to realize how special you are. As you focus on your gifts and special unique abilities, you will find confidence in yourself. As you educate yourself, you will gain competence, and that brings confidence. You will cherish your uniqueness and your differences and feel less threatened by the accomplishments of others. You won't feel the need to blame events and people for your weaknesses, and yet, you won't feel overwhelmed by them either. You will be able to overcome bad habits and be more honest with yourself.

As you gain spiritual, emotional, and academic knowledge, you will begin to see the woman you can become. The woman you and Heavenly Father discussed before you left home. You will feel the self-esteem that comes through knowledge of the "mysteries and peaceable things . . . that which bringeth joy."

JOY OF THE HOLY GHOST

"For the kingdom of God is . . . righteousness, and peace, and joy in the Holy Ghost."

—Romans 14:17

When my friend Linda came to see me, one of the greatest worries was that she did not feel the Holy Ghost in her life. She said that a few times she thought it was the Holy Ghost but wasn't sure. She also wondered why He was so important.

Why is He so important?

Years ago, when my husband was an Elder's Quorum President, he came home one night after interviewing a man who had been excommunicated. What he told me that night changed my life forever. I only wish someone could have told me this when I was in my youth.

Maybe they did, and I wasn't listening. Are you listening?

Without revealing the man's identity, my husband told me that this man had been excommunicated and was trying to be rebaptized. He was finding it hard because, as he said, "I never realized how much the Holy Ghost influenced me on a day-to-day basis until He was taken away!"

I was stunned. What did that man mean? Having been baptized when eight, I had never really known life without the Holy Ghost. I thought He was there to tell you the Church was true, which person to marry, when to move, what to study in school, what dark alley to avoid; but what did this man mean "on a day-to-day basis"?

So I began an experiment. For a few days I gave strict attention to all the thoughts and ideas that came to my mind. I would ask myself, was this my own thought or was this the Holy

Ghost? It was amazing to me how much He really did influence me on a day-to-day basis, and it was amazingly easy to tell it was Him once I paid attention.

Let me share a few "day-to-day" experiences so that you will understand how important He is to our lives.

One day at school my daughter's classmate said to her, "Let's tell the teacher we lost our lunch money so she'll give us more money. Then we'll have money all week for popsicles. When we get home, we'll tell our moms we lost our lunch money, and they'll give us enough to pay the teacher back."

My daughter said she thought about that for a minute. She really wanted a popsicle. Then she looked down at her hands and her C.T.R. ring and "something" said to her, "Choose the Right." She told her friend that was not the right thing to do and walked away.

That "something" was the Holy Ghost.

A friend of mine lives in a big city in an apartment with five other girls. The city is full of crime and danger. Their neighborhood had been having a lot of robberies and rapes the past few months, and this worried my friend because her roommates were careless about locking the door.

The door would not close unless you pulled it hard. The lock would not snap into place without a good, hard shove on the door. In a hurry most of the time, the girls wouldn't pull it hard enough. My friend would often wake up in the morning or come home at night and find the door slightly ajar.

She tried everything; discussions, notes on the bathroom mirror, screaming and yelling. Nothing worked; the girls remained careless.

One day at work, while busy typing, into her thoughts came three words—"oil the lock." Where did that silly thought come from, she wondered. As she thought about it, she decided to try it. On her way home she bought a can of oil and oiled the lock. Immediately the door slid closed and locked easily into place!

That "silly thought" was the Holy Ghost.

My husband had been working hard all day in the yard. There had been weeding and lawnmowing and carrying bags of seed and fertilizer all day. We had to go to a meeting that night, and he was in a hurry. Covered with mud and fertilizer, he did not want to track that into the house so he took off his shoes by the back door to clean off later. They were brand-new work shoes, and he had paid a lot of money for them. He paused there, and the "thought" came into his mind to take them inside. But he decided to leave them because he was in a hurry and would get them later.

He forgot all about it, and the next morning he discovered one missing. Searching the entire yard brought nothing. He realized a dog had probably carried it away forever.

That "thought" had been the Holy Ghost.

One of my friends was assigned to be the visiting teacher of an inactive sister. This inactive girl would not let her in the house. But month after month my friend tried to start a friendship with her because she wanted to do her level best as a visiting teacher.

The week of this girl's birthday came, and my friend decided to bake her a cake. This might be a way to break the ice, she thought. She went to the store to buy a cake mix, and as she looked over the boxes on the shelf the "thought" of German Chocolate Cake came into mind. She thought, "Well, I've never made a German Chocolate Cake before, but I guess I could try."

She left the store without a mix and went home to bake a German Chocolate Cake. Carefully she followed directions in her cookbook, and the result was a beautiful, delicious cake. Excited about her accomplishment, she rushed over to deliver it to her inactive sister.

The door opened, and my friend said, "Happy Birthday! This is my first attempt at a German Chocolate Cake, and it came out perfect. I want you to have it for your birthday."

Tears welled up in the girl's eyes, and she said to my friend, "How did you know? German Chocolate Cake is my favorite.

No one has ever done this for me before. Please, please come in."

That "thought" in the grocery store was from the Holy Ghost.

Several summers ago while my children were swimming, I needed to run to a neighbor's house a few streets away. I would only be gone a few minutes, so I told the children they could stay in the pool until I came back. My children are good swimmers, but their cousin who was visiting was not. They were playing in the shallow end with a rubber raft, and I thought they would be all right.

I started out the door and down the walk when the thought came into my mind to take the rubber raft out of the pool. Where did that silly thought come from, I wondered and walked on my way. But I stopped a moment later, realizing it was probably the Holy Ghost and returned to take the raft out of the pool. Five minutes later when I returned, all was well. I could only assume that if I'd left the raft in, my niece may have drifted into the deep end and been in danger. I don't know why; I only know the thought was from the Holy Ghost.

And just last week I was busy working when suddenly the impression came to me to call a lady in my ward. I thought that was a good idea, and I would do it later—I was too busy then. But I realized it was the Holy Ghost and called her right then. She answered and broke into tears, "Oh, Anita, I needed to talk to someone this very moment. Thank you for calling." She thanked me, and I was thankful for the Holy Ghost.

There are so many "day-to-day" influences I could share, but they would fill a book alone. As you learn to pay attention and listen, you will find His influence all day long. Have faith and patience; it takes practice to learn to listen to the Holy Ghost. Practice means listening and *obeying* the voice! Listening and obeying strengthens your testimony of the Holy Ghost, and He becomes more familiar and more real to you! And that, my friends, is indeed joy!

How important is the Holy Ghost in your daily life? Exactly

what is His mission? How often does he prompt and influence you?

Let me explain why the Holy Ghost is necessary for us in order to live with joy in this earth.

Heavenly Father and Heavenly Mother made us just like them. We have all the body parts and organs and tissues that they have. We are made just like Them. We also have all the senses they have (sight, smell, hearing, tasting, touch) and all of their characteristics. Characteristics are things like love, sympathy, patience, and so on.

We are just like them—except for one huge difference. They are perfect. Their bodies and organs and tissues are perfect. Their senses and characteristics are perfect. We don't really understand how complex that truly is, but perfect means *flawless, total, complete, finished.* That's why I said we use only two percent of our brains, and God uses 100 percent. We have all that they have because we inherited characteristics from our Heavenly Parents like we inherit certain features from our Mortal Parents. But in mortal life we are like Them in an incomplete stage. We are in the "rough."

So how does a person in the "rough" perfect those organs, senses, characteristics, and become like God?

That is the role of the Holy Ghost! The Holy Ghost has the power to come to our level and help us get to God's level.

How can He do that?

Let me list twelve ways that the Holy Ghost helps us to become like Heavenly Father and Heavenly Mother. Pay close attention and look for these in your own life.

1. Through Him we can receive answers to our prayers. He can bear witness to the truth of the answers we receive.

2. He helps you understand your potential by sharpening your intelligence. He helps you understand that you are a daughter of God. Joseph Smith called it, "pure intelligence flowing through you." The Holy Ghost

places thoughts in our minds to help us learn, to protect us, and to comfort us.

3. He helps you control your passions and appetites (eating, sleeping, morals, etc.).

4. He inspires you to remember the kind of spirit you are. A righteous soul that stepped forward in the preexistence to be counted on the Lord's side.

5. He helps you to recall the gifts you were given in the preexistence. He helps you "feel familiar" with them and that helps you develop your talents.

6. He helps you recall feelings from the preexistence. That's why when people hear gospel teachings they seem familiar. We know we heard them before we came to earth. By the power of the Holy Ghost you can know the Church is true. In fact, you can know the truth of *all* things.

7. He inspires you to goodness, kindness, and love by making our hearts swell within us and feel tender.

8. He actually makes us beautiful. Once someone asked me why all Mormons looked so clean; was it a special soap they used? When the Spirit is within a person, they actually look clean and radiate beauty.

9. He helps us feel health and strength. Doctors are now saying 85 percent of illness is caused by "thinking" about it. The Holy Ghost can help us control our thoughts.

10. The Holy Ghost will aid you in having more personality and being more relaxed socially. The companionship of the Holy Ghost gives you self-confidence.

11. The Holy Ghost can make you calm and soften you. He can arm you with courage in the face of problems. He can fill your heart with peace, even in the middle of turmoil.

12. He gives us joy. As we maintain closeness with Him, we feel glad to be alive!

He is there, the still small voice, if we will just listen and then OBEY! What good is it to have the gift of the Holy Ghost if we don't use it? We must also live worthy of this gift by obeying the commandments.

There are some good guidelines to follow in understanding how the Holy Ghost works within us:

When You Have The Spirit:

1. You feel happy, calm, and clear-minded.
2. You feel generous.
3. Nobody can offend you.
4. You wouldn't mind everybody seeing what you're doing.
5. You are eager to be with people and want to make them happy.
6. You are glad when others succeed.
7. You are glad to attend your meetings and participate in church activities.
8. You feel like praying.
9. You wish you could keep all the Lord's commandments.
10. You feel "in control." You don't overeat or sleep too much. You don't feel uncontrollably drawn to sensational entertainment, lose your temper, or feel uncontrollable passions or desires.
11. You think about the Savior often, and you want to know Him better.
12. You feel confident and are glad to be alive.

When You Don't Have The Spirit:

1. You feel unhappy, depressed, confused, and frustrated.
2. You feel possessive, self-centered, or resentful of demands made on you.

3. You are easily offended.

4. You become secretive and evasive.

5. You avoid people, especially members of your family, and you are critical of family members and Church authorities.

6. You envy or resent the successes of others.

7. You don't want to go to church, go home teaching, or take the sacrament. You wish you had another church job or no job at all.

8. You don't want to pray.

9. You find the commandments bothersome, restricting, or senseless.

10. You feel emotions and appetites so strongly that you fear you cannot control them, i.e., hate, jealousy, anger, lust, hunger, fatigue.

11. You rarely think of the Savior. He seems irrelevant to your life, or worse, part of a confusing system that seems to work against you.

12. You get discouraged easily and wonder if life is really worth it.

—Ensign, August 1978, pp. 32-33

The Holy Ghost is the vehicle by which you may travel from one level of faith and righteousness to another, until you eventually arrive at the very gates of Godhood. He is a comforter, a companion, a healer, a teacher, a guardian, and a counselor. He is a friend! He will encourage you and inspire you all along the way. He will help you take that first step. If you will just seek Him, live worthy of Him by striving to obey the commandments; if you will watch and listen, He will be there.

I had my first experience with the Holy Ghost when I was seven years old. I was baptized on my eighth birthday, and my testimony came a few months prior to that, so this must have occurred in the winter of 1954.

My mother had joined the Church about a year and a half

before, with my father following her on Valentine's Day, 1953. The gospel had changed their lives and indirectly changed mine. But I continually asked my mother, "How do you know for sure it's true?" She taught me the principle of the Holy Ghost and her experiences of a burning in her heart. She was so convinced the Church was true that I thought it had to be; at seven years old my mother always knew the right answers! But I desired that burning in my heart. I desired to know for myself.

Primary was after school—I think on Thursday. Our class met on the stage behind the drawn curtains. It was cold back there. I remember pulling my sweater around me. Our class was preparing us for baptism, and the discussion that day had something to do with baptism. But the conversation turned to the *Book of Mormon,* and the thought went through my mind, "How do I know the *Book of Mormon* is true?" And then came the burning in my heart, and I knew.

A few months later, when I stepped into the waters of baptism, I knew I was joining the Lord's church.

I remember the white dress Mother made me. We were going to be sealed as a family in the Mesa Temple later in the month, and she had made her girls matching temple dresses. She finished mine early so I could also be baptized in it. As I descended into that warm water, and my dad held out his brown hands to escort me, my heart pounded. I pushed the little dress down in the water with Dad's help. He clasped my arm, and I his, and then I heard the words that were music to my ears: "Anita Rodriquez, having been commissioned of Jesus Christ, I baptize you in the name of the Father and of the Son and of the Holy Ghost, Amen."

As I came up out of the water, a warm glow seemed to permeate my soul, and I felt a renewing of my body. Someone said, "Anita, you are glowing," and in my soul I felt it, even the burning in my heart.

At age eight I lacked the maturity and vocabulary to express that event as I can now. The time, the years, the words have all changed, but the heart and those feelings have not. From the heart and mind of an innocent and tender eight-year-old child to that of a thirty-seven-year-old woman; the Holy Ghost is real, positive, and still my friend.

And He is a friend to all of us who invite Him to be our friend. Even if you think you don't have a friend in the whole world, you do. It is Him. He is always there, but it is up to you to welcome Him.

I promise you that you can make every decision correctly if you learn to follow the guidance of the Holy Ghost. This you can do if you follow the roadmap the Lord has marked. You will need to learn to give up your own feelings and give in to the promptings of the Holy Ghost.

There is hardly a joy more wonderful than knowing you have a friend you can count on!

JOY OF MISSIONARY WORK

"And now, if your joy will be great with one soul that you have brought unto me into the kingdom of my Father, how great will be your joy if you should bring many souls unto me."

—D&C 18:16

Friendshipping and being friendshipped are really some of life's choicest experiences, aren't they? There is nothing like good friends to share good fun, or even problems, at any age. When I was in my teens, I dreaded doing anything alone. I needed my friends to help me grow and learn. Friends give us strength. And likewise we can give strengths to our friends, too. To have good friends we must learn to be good friends.

I would like to share the following counsel that is in my patriarchal blessing:

> Learn to choose good companions and do not become contaminated with the sins of the world.

Why do you think that these two statements are in the same sentence? Because bad companions can influence us toward wrong choices. Part of being a good friend is to be a good example. But the other part of being a good friend is to pick good friends.

My young sisters, I know how hard it is to be alone and how much better it is to have friends around you. But always remember that *it is better to be alone than in the company of those who would lead you astray!*

Being a good friend means building and raising those around you, too. It is an eternal principle that *when you build and raise others, you build and raise yourself.*

When Linda came to see me, she found that this had been

missing in her life. She had spent so much time with thoughts turned inward that she had not even seen opportunities to share the gospel or build others. She didn't have any good friends because she had not been a good friend.

One of the greatest ways to be a friend is to be a missionary for Jesus Christ. Being a missionary means being an example of how the gospel has helped you face your problems and disappointments. It also means to share how happy it has made you knowing who you are and why you are here and where you are going. You can do this by your example. By honoring your parents, by being honest, by doing your best, and by even bearing your testimony. Bearing your testimony is a great cleansing experience.

Several years ago there was a young man who desired to go on a mission. But he was slow of speech, had a learning disability, and was unable to memorize the discussions. But he desired to go on a mission. Now this young man had everything going against him in the eyes of the world. He was handicapped, he was unedu-cated, he was slow of speech, and he came from a very poor family. He could have groveled in his poor self-image. He could have said, "Well, I don't have any self-esteem so how could I possibly build or raise anybody else's? They need to build and raise me!" Instead, he chose to serve his Savior by going on a mission. He entered the mission field at age 26. He never did learn the discussions in the two years he was out. Not once could he even memorize one scripture or quote anything. But so great was his testimony and so powerful was his conviction that Jesus is the Christ and that this church is the Church of Jesus Christ that the missionaries throughout the mission wanted him to bear his testimony to their investigators. His testimony was responsible for touching the lives of hundreds and seeing hundreds of people enter into the waters of baptism. He left his mission with a feeling of accomplishment and a feeling and a sense of self-worth and self-esteem. He left the mission field with lots of *good* friends. It is an eternal principle that when you build and raise others, you build and raise yourself.

Elder Vaughn J. Featherstone remembers how the missionary work of his friends and associates brought him into the gospel.

At about that same time we couldn't afford much clothing, either. I had a pair of shoes that I'd wear to church. They weren't the best shoes. They had holes in the bottom sole, so I'd cut out pieces of cardboard and slide then in as an insole. When I went to church, I would sit with both feet flat on the floor; I didn't want to raise one leg and have someone see 'Quaker Oats' across the bottom of my shoe. I'd go off to church that way, and everything was fine until those shoes wore out. Then I didn't know what I would do. I remember it was Saturday, and I thought, 'I've got to go to church. Over at church I am somebody. They really care about me.' I remember thinking that through, and I went to a little box of shoes some neighbors had given us. I went through them, but I could find only one pair of shoes that would fit me. They were a pair of nurse's shoes. I thought, 'How can I wear those? They'll laugh me to scorn over at church.' And so I decided I wouldn't wear them, and I wouldn't go to church.

I went through that night, and the next morning I knew I had to go! I had to wear the nurse's shoes. There was a great attraction over at church. I had to go. I decided what to do. I would run over there very early and sit down close to the front before anybody got there. I thought, 'I'll put my feet back under the pew so no one can see them, and then I'll wait till everyone leaves. After they're gone, I'll come running home half an hour later or something.' That was my plan. I dashed over to church half an hour early, and it worked. Nobody was there. I put my feet back under the bench. Pretty soon everyone came in, and then all of a sudden someone announced: 'We will now separate for classes.' I had forgotten we had to go to class. I was terrified! The ushers came down the aisle, and as they got to our row, everybody got up and left. But I just sat there. I couldn't move. I knew I couldn't move for fear someone would see my shoes. The pressure was intense. That whole meeting seemed to stop and wait until I moved, so I had to move. I got up and followed the class downstairs.

I think I learned the greatest lesson I have ever learned in my life that day. I went downstairs to class, and the teacher had us sit in a big half circle. Each of the shoes felt two feet in diameter. I can't tell you how embarrassed I was. I watched, but, do you know, not one of those eight and nine-year-old children in that class laughed at me. Not one of them looked at me. No one pointed at my shoes. My teacher didn't look. I was watching everyone to see if anyone was looking at me, and I didn't hear a word of the lesson. When it was finally over, I dashed home, went in the house and thought to myself, 'Thank goodness nobody saw them.' How ridiculous! Of course they saw those nurse's shoes that I had to wear to church. But they had the fine instinct not to laugh.

I guess the Lord knew that I had had all the pressure I could possibly take, that I couldn't take one particle more of pressure. I believe that all of us will find in our lives that some of our obstacles turn into advantages and great blessings.

What I am saying is that if the Lord will take a scroungy little kid like that, who had to wear nurse's shoes to church and had to go and beg for groceries, and if he will make him a high councilor or a stake president or the second counselor in the Presiding Bishopric or a member of the First Quorum of the Seventy, can you believe what he would do for you? (Featherstone, *Charity Never Faileth*, Bookcraft, Salt Lake City, Utah.)

And what will the Lord do for you as you live up to all you have been taught? What will He do for you as you stay valiant in your testimony?

Do you realize that you are all He has? In this world of wickedness there are only a few He can count on. His people are only a few compared to this huge world. And of His people, His youth are going to have to be the best. The scriptures talk about the wicked who will be burned at the Lord's coming. Who are they? You have also been told that you are the generation to prepare His coming. I assume that means many of you will meet Him. That means the wicked who will be burned might be people you know today. Young people today whose hearts are growing cold and hard and who will turn far away from the truth! If you are indeed a royal, righteous generation, it is because you need to be! Your wicked opposition will be the most intense this world has ever known.

But somewhere out there, among your friends, are more just like you. They need you. The Lord needs you to find them. You young people are the only future the Lord has. There are others who would come "Home" except they know not where to find it. It is up to you to lead them, by example, by courage, and by testimony.

And what will the Lord do for you? He has promised you crowns of glory and joy forever and ever.

Being a good friend means loving another person and wanting good things for them. There is such a great joy in seeing someone you love come into the gospel. There is great joy in knowing they have found the road to eternal perspective and can see the potential in themselves. There is great joy in knowing that friendship will be forever and ever.

> And now, if your joy will be great with one soul that you have brought unto me into the kingdom of my Father, how great will be your joy if you should bring many souls unto me!
>
> —D&C 18:16

JOY OF REPENTANCE

"I say unto you, that likewise joy shall be in heaven over one sinner that repenteth, more than over ninety and nine just persons, which need no repentance."

—Luke 15:7

A lie that Satan tries to tell us is "It's my life, and I'll do what I want!" "If I want to hurt myself, I will; I'm not hurting anybody else."

That's a lie he wants us to believe, because each of us is part of the great family of God. Each of us is part of the whole kingdom. What we do either magnifies or marks the whole picture.

I know a young woman who let Satan convince her that it was her life and that she could do whatever she pleased. If she wanted to hurt herself, it didn't matter; she wasn't affecting anyone else. How wrong! She got involved with drugs and alcohol. She abused her body and her mind. She had an illegitimate baby. She ended up living at home, with her father supporting her and the baby until she was almost 38 years old. In her path of self-destruction she left financial and emotional burdens on her family and friends.

Once we are buried in that kind of thinking, Satan makes us believe there is no need for repentance; or that we are too "far away" to repent. We are never too far away to repent. Repentance is a miracle. Every time we sin, we lose a little of our eternal perspective and lose a little more joy. Repentance is a miracle because even though sin eats at us little by little, repentance can make us feel well and whole again.

This is a true story told by Elder Featherstone:

One day a woman came to my church office. She leaned across the desk and said, 'Elder Featherstone, I have carried a transgression on my heart for thirty-four years. I cannot carry it one more step. But I know how tender-hearted you are, and I wouldn't add one particle of a burden to your soul.' I said, 'My dear sister, before you go on, let me share with you a principle of the gospel. When you take a burden off your soul, it is lifted from the priesthood leader's soul also.' She said, 'I know I will be cast out, I know I will be excommunicated, but does it have to be forever? Thirty-four years ago, before my first husband and I were married, I had an abortion. Since that time, I have felt like a murderess. It was my husband's idea, and I did not resist it. Later we got married. He was unfaithful constantly during the first two years of our marriage. I finally divorced him and have since remarried a wonderful man who is a convert to the Church. He knows everything, and he still wants to be sealed to me. Elder Featherstone, do you think that either in time or in eternity we can be sealed together? I know I will be cast out, but does it have to be forever?' The tears flowed down her cheeks. I had known this woman and thought she was one of the most Christlike women I had ever met. She always baked bread, rolls, or cookies for the people in her neighborhood. Whenever they had a ward party and the Relief Society sisters cleaned up, she always scrubbed the floor. She said that she didn't feel worthy to stand by them and do the dishes after what she had done; she felt worthy only to scrub the floor where they walked. She told me that she had never gossiped about anyone else. 'How could I,' she said, 'after what I had done?'

I listened to her confession, humbled to tears, and told her, 'I have never had a case of abortion before. I will need to write to President Kimball, President of the Council of the Twelve, and get his counsel.'

I wrote to President Kimball and shared the entire story. I told him she was one of the most Christlike women I had known and that she was willing to submit to any decision he would have for her. Two weeks later I received his response. I called the sister and asked her to meet me at the office as soon as she could. When I arrived, she was already there. Her eyes were red, and she was pale. I know she must have been on her knees several times after my call, asking for mercy.

Again I sat across the desk from her and said, 'I do not want to keep you waiting one second longer. We are not even going to stop for prayer. Let me read you President Kimball's letter.'

It read:

> Dear Elder Featherstone:
>
> You inquired about a woman who had been involved in an abortion thirty-four years ago. From the way you describe her, it sounds as though she has long since repented. You may tell her, on behalf of the Church, she is forgiven.
>
> After a thorough and searching interview, you may issue this sweet sister a temple recommend so she can go to the temple and be sealed to her present husband.

If the Savior had been sitting where the woman sat, I would not have felt any closer to Him. I believe that is exactly what He would have said. A great burden had been lifted from the heart of this good woman. She wept with relief and joy. To this day I do not remember who the woman was. (Vaughn Featherstone, *Purity of Heart*, Bookcraft.)

No matter where you have been in the past, or even where you are today, the only thing that matters is that you are going in the right direction, that you are on the right road.

The miracle of repentance is real. It is real joy to feel that unburdening of a sin. And Father in Heaven is as loving and eager to forgive as was this mother of an LDS youth who served time in prison for robbery:

> We appreciated your testimony and were thrilled at the goals you have set for yourself spiritually. The law of repentance is such a beautiful part of the gospel. It is good that you remember the past mistakes but don't dwell on them. You can be an inspiration and help many people to make good decisions. You can give hope and courage to those who are going through similar things. The Lord permitted Satan to test you just so far to help you be the humble repentant spirit that you are now. We feel blessed to have you for our son and are proud of you. I know that as long as you continue to grow in the gospel, you will have the

Lord's strength and power to overcome anything you should. We all love you.

Love,
Mother

This mother forgave and loved her son as though he had never sinned. How much greater is your Heavenly Father's love which is perfect?

If you are suffering, turn to Him. If you are weak, He is not. If you are afraid, He is not. If you feel alone, He is there, lovingly and eagerly waiting to hear your quiet secret prayer.

How do you repent? How does it start? And how do you know it is accepted by Father in Heaven? The process is simple:

1. You feel guilt. You know you have done something wrong.
2. You feel as though you have offended Heavenly Father. You feel sorry, with a broken heart and in humility.
3. You discontinue the sin.
4. You confess it, either to Heavenly Father in secret prayer, and if it is of moral nature, to the bishop also.
5. Pay back or make it up if possible.

There is no greater relief than unburdening our sins to the Lord. He is eager to forgive us. He waits with loving gentleness to forgive us.

Sometimes we are afraid to repent because we condemn ourselves instead of condemning the sin. It is good to sorrow for what we have done wrong, but not to feel worthless because of the sin. Satan wants you to believe that. If that were true, then Jesus suffered in Gethsemane for *nothing*, because none of us would be worth it! But we are; we are His sheep, and He is our Shepherd. He wants us safely home, even the lost lambs.

I seriously started repenting when I was about twelve years old. I don't remember any real problems then, but I remember being more aware of wrong-doings. Looking back over the years, I find that for over 25 years I have been repenting for the same things.

That doesn't mean I haven't made progress. In fact, it's exciting to look back and see some shiny, sparkling places on the "old rock." But basically it's the same "old rock" that needs a lot of polishing. We came here to earth with these weaknesses and the charge to overcome them. It will take us a lifetime of repenting. So be patient with yourself, you cannot become perfect overnight. Perfection is a long, slow process. Perfection is not an event!

How often should you repent?

I have a friend who owns a Rolls-Royce. He has had this car for two years. It is so bright and shiny that you can look into any part of it and see yourself as a mirror. And yet, the car has never been waxed since he bought it two years ago! In fact, it hasn't been washed for almost two months now! Yet it is as shiny and new as the day he bought it.

His secret is that every morning he wipes the car down with a clean damp chamois. Because the car doesn't need waxing and washing constantly, it keeps its fresh, new appearance.

So it is with us. If we repent every single day, we keep our spirits in better tune with our Heavenly Father. We are better able to measure our progress when we return and report to Him. We are better able to experience the sweet joy that comes from being honest with Him. We are better able to forsake our wrong forever. Through repentance we can see eternal perspective.

Repentance is a miracle. It is a miracle that brings joy!

JOY OF TRIALS

"Ye shall be sorrowful, but your sorrow shall be turned into joy."
—John 16:20

How could there be any joy in sorrow!
May I share this letter from a sweet sixteen-year-old girl who lives in Utah:

Dear Sister Canfield,
My name is Marilee, and I am sixteen years old.
I think a healthy self-esteem is probably the most important single quality a person can possess.
A healthy self-image is something I am still struggling for. But I have come a long way. I was born with a severe case of club feet. The doctors told my parents that if I hadn't been born today, I would probably have never walked. I was put in casts up to my hips until I was six months old. When I was eleven, I had a series of operations which gave me a permanent correction. I can remember so vividly laying in that hospital bed screaming in pain. I could not understand why I had to go through this. Now I do. Through that experience I am able to empathize with people more and because of the severe pain and agony, I became closer to Heavenly Father.
At the end of my eleventh year, having shed my last cast three months earlier, my dad was called to be a mission president. I had always been an outgoing person and had lots of friends. I loved school and being involved. But when I moved, my new school had a full length mirror. For the first time in my life I watched myself walk in front of that mirror with other kids and realized that I was different. I was rather deformed. As I walked in front of that mirror that difference became bigger and bigger. Every time I saw myself I would get nauseated and felt a little dizzy. I started to find other ways to get to my class, even though it made me late. I began feeling sorry for other people who had to look at me. The outgoing person I once was became a bitter but quiet, timid person who was afraid to answer a question in class. I took it for granted that

everyone hated me as much as I hated myself. My parents mistook my quiet, inward behavior as a sour attitude. I thought seriously about suicide but didn't have the guts to go through with it. Through a series of events, I decided it was time for a change. Although it was really tough, I tried to act as though I already had a healthy self-image. I improved my clothes which had gone downhill as fast as my self-image, tried to be outgoing and friendly, turned my usual sour expression to a smile, and acted as if I had an exuberant *joy* of life. Although on the inside I still felt hurt and angry, I didn't let it show. For two years I tried this. I am beginning to feel that *joy* of living I thought was lost forever. I have a close relationship with Heavenly Father. (I became very close to Him since I followed the line of reasoning that if He created me, He was stuck with me.)

I still have a way to go, but I'm happy with the progress I've made. I can help other people because of my experiences.

I think a healthy self-image is also a thanks to God. He created us, and when we love ourselves, we are telling Him that He did a good job!

There are lessons to be learned in our trials. Lessons that we probably think we don't need, but Heavenly Father knows what we need to become more humble, more teachable, so that we can learn to become like Him, so that we can understand joy!

Many people rise to greatness not in spite of their trials but because of their trials.

Helen Keller should be an inspiration to women everywhere, handicapped either physically or by their own weaknesses. Inspiration is the wrong word to describe her. She is a *rock*. I love her because of her life. What prompted my interest in Helen Keller was a picture of her in the encyclopedia. When I saw it, I was astonished by the look on her face. She did not look blind. There was a definite sparkle in her eyes, a look of depth, intelligence, and recognition. Eyes are the reflection of the soul. Every ounce of her soul was reflected in her eyes and in her whole face. As I read books about her work and thoughts and accomplishments, I felt her indomitable spirit and her enthusiasm for life. She was responsible for many of the improvements for the blind.

She graduated from Radcliff with honors. She was active on the staffs of many foundations for the blind and deaf. She travelled to underdeveloped and war-ravaged countries and helped establish better conditions for the blind. She lectured in America and in twenty-five other countries. She aided and comforted servicemen who had been blinded in World War II. She wrote many books which have been translated into more than fifty languages. Wherever she went, she brought new courage to thousands of blind persons and inspired millions of others with her zeal. She never married; she never had any children, but she influenced literally millions.

She could have said, "I'm deaf, dumb, and blind. What can I do? Who can I help?" She could even have said, "Why me? Others owe me help." But no! Helen Keller thought the opposite. She knew the word joy! Helen Keller—blind, deaf, and dumb—said, "I have found life so beautiful!"

Remember in the *Book of Mormon,* Father Lehi told his son, Jacob, that in order to know joy we must learn sorrow, too. Sorrow is a part of learning. But being human we just don't want to suffer.

Heavenly Father told us these things are for our own good. He has explained that some of these hard disappointments and trials of life help to make us stronger. It's like the rubber band principle. When a rubber band is laying on the table by itself in the exact size and shape it was made, it serves no purpose. But when it is stretched and pulled, it suddenly becomes of value.

Unless you are stretched and proven, how can you ever know all that you can become? When life is comfortable and relaxed for us, we don't have to stretch ourselves. We don't have to reach deep inside ourselves for more power and self-control. When we reach deep inside, we discover our potential and find out how strong we can be!

When we lived with Heavenly Father and Heavenly Mother, we wanted to be like them more than anything else in all eternity. We knew that coming to earth would be the way it could be done. We knew we would get bodies like Theirs and go through experiences that would make us more like Them. We were glad to come because more than anything we wanted to be like Them. We were willing to pay the price!

But then we came and found out that suffering isn't easy, and the price to be paid is a hard one. But it will be worth it! You just have to believe that! If it wasn't worth it, we wouldn't have to work so hard for it.

I asked my daughter Ashley if I could share a part of her patriarchal blessing with you. It says, "There will be many trials in your life." It then goes on to talk about the weight of those trials in her life. Being Ashley's mother, I don't want her to suffer, and yet when I read the promise that follows, I am sure that Ashley will grow in might and power because of her trials. It says, "As you view all things in light of the spirit of the gospel, you shall be comforted, and you will know with *a greater assurance that the Lord loves you* . . ."

To me that means that my Ashley's sorrow will be turned into joy!

And so it is with each of us. There is no way to escape the trials, *we need them.* Trials are universal, but our reactions to them are individual. They will either inspire or bury us. The choice is ours.

But there is the promise and comfort that Father will bind up our wounds and love and comfort us. That is how sorrow is turned into joy!

JOY OF MOTHERHOOD

"... and to be a joyful mother of children."

—Psalms 113:9

One of a young woman's greatest dreams and expectations is to marry in the temple and become a wife and mother. When I was in my teens, I, too, often dreamed about growing up, meeting the right man, and falling madly in love. I often pictured myself in the most gorgeous white, satin wedding gown covered with lace and pearls. It's a dream all young girls expect to come true.

The Lord has planted in the hearts of girls the desire to be mothers. We have been chosen to bear the vessels of the Lord. We have not only been made physically able to be mothers, the Lord made us spiritually able, too. Our Mother in Heaven was a beautiful and *perfect* example for us. Our Spirits ache to be like Her. It is a longing and a remembering deep within us. Yes, our minds have forgotten our former home, but our spirits will never forget.

And so my young sisters, it is important that we listen to our spirits, our hearts, and prepare for motherhood.

First on the list is living a pure and chaste life, living worthy of the Kingdom of God. Next is finding a worthy companion whom we can marry in the temple.

Now these principles have been taught to you repeatedly by your parents and teachers. Everywhere you turn you are being taught the principle of Celestial Marriage.

My purpose is to warn you.

I have a filing cabinet drawer full of letters from young women in their early twenties who did not listen and now find themselves very troubled. The ideal seems to be that we grow up, get married to Prince Charming, have chubby pink babies, hang lacy curtains in our windows, and look into the sunset.

Do not be misled by starry-eyed ideas!

Ask yourself why there are so many divorces. Why do marriages fail? Why do dreams crumble and fall apart? Well, the reasons are many, but a lot of it has to do with poor judgement. And we make poor judgements when we haven't studied the facts and sought confirmation for our decisions through the power of the Holy Ghost.

When I was single, I had a list of qualifications that I thought would make a good husband. They were:

1. Handsome
2. Older than me
3. Religious
4. Able to earn a lot of money
5. Likes airplanes
6. Likes art
7. Likes to dance
8. Sharp dresser

I had some pretty glamourous boyfriends then. I was in my late twenties and dated mostly older and successful men. One was a prominent dentist, one a wealthy and famous doctor, one owned an airline company, and one was a successful businessman.

I went to the nicest restaurants, rode in expensive cars, and was given beautiful presents. One time my date drove me to the airport and flew me in a private jet to another state for dinner! The dancing and dining were fun and glamourous until the hour came to go home. None of these men were Latter-day Saints and had worldly ways. I thought that there were no men my age in the Church left to marry. I preferred the company of nonmember men until the hour came to take me home.

It was the same scene every date. Before he would leave, he would do his best to make me compromise my standards. Over and over I had to defend my morals. Eventually, I dreaded the end of a date. Why did I date them? Because of the glamour! And besides, I was strong enough to resist, nothing would happen to me. I had been taught right.

Do you see how Satan was wearing me down?

Yes, I had been taught, but I wasn't listening anymore.

And then one night I listened. I listened because the voice came loud and clear:

"Anita, if you want a Cadillac, stop looking in the junkyard!"

The voice pierced me to the heart! It was right! I did want a cadillac, I really did. And I knew then that I had been looking in the junkyard.

As I reevaluated my goals and values, I wrote a new list.

1. A man committed to God with his heart, might, mind, and strength.

And that was the entire list.

I knew if I ever found a man like that he would be handsome because he would be pure. He would be mature and able to provide a good living for his family because he would be a hard worker, and he would love all the beauties of his Father in Heaven.

I found him.

I found him because I started listening again.

I found him because I looked in the right place—with the Saints of God.

I am saying to you what I tell my own daughters. Do not think you can sit in your classes and listen to your teachers tell you about the steps to a happy celestial marriage and then leave thinking you can skip some of those steps!

That would be like trying to climb a ladder with rungs missing. It would be a struggle to get to the top, and some would fall to the ground and be too hurt to try again! *You cannot skip any steps!*

Many sisters become mothers soon after marrying. Remember, your husband will be the father of your children. You will be their mother. Will you be prepared?

I love my children. Words cannot describe the joy of holding a beautiful, new baby in your arms. May I share something my mother wrote to me as I was turning twelve and entering Beehives:

> Sweet are the words that fall upon the ear of a new mother, as a white figure bends, watching, listening for response to the announcement, 'Say, do you know you have a little girl?'
>
> At that great moment, those are the *only* words in the English language, for even their meaning nearly surpasses all understanding.
>
> Unspeakable joy? This only feebly describes what I knew when the little bundle that was you squirmed and kicked as I held you for the first time.
>
> Unspeakable joy? These words will be better understood when one day you experience the soft touch of your first babe.
>
> I pray that you will always keep the standards of the Church, Anita dear, that you might know that fullness of *joy* we are told can be ours in the Celestial Kingdom . . . and this, truly *unspeakable.*

To be a joyful mother! What an exciting prospect!

Our last baby is adopted. She came when I found that I was unable to have anymore children.

For several months we knew that we were going to adopt a baby. We began to make plans and talk about boys' names and girls' names. We went window shopping in baby stores, resisting purchases until we knew for sure what the baby would be. Since we had two boys and one girl, everyone was hoping for a girl to even out the house! But we would be glad for whoever came.

During these months of planning and expecting, I would find myself wondering, "How long will it take me to feel like the baby is mine?" Many times I asked myself that question and worried that I would feel distant from the child.

I decided that it would probably take about six months. Six months was the law for adoption to be legal. Six months and we could take it to the temple to be sealed. Yes, I thought, when we take the baby to the temple, then I will feel it is mine!

The day came that the baby was born. We were so excited, a

little girl! We could hardly wait to hold her. We drove to the store and bought diapers, a gown and blanket, and delivered them to the agents who would pick up our little girl.

We paced the floor, the excitement mounted, the hours dragged by like days. And then we saw a car coming. It was them! Suddenly the noisy room became absolutely quiet. We could see them coming up the walk. My heart pounded. I could hear it. I was afraid!

Would I love her?

Would she seem like mine?

How long would it really take to love her?

We opened the door, and I saw the little squirming bundle. They came right over to me and placed her in my arms. Tears welled in my eyes, and I could hardly contain my joy! At the moment she was placed in my arms, I saw her not adult to infant, or even mother to daughter; it was *sister to sister!*

And I knew we had known each other before.

We are all sisters, we always have been, and we always will be. Your mothers were perhaps your very closest sisters in our Heavenly Home. And they were willing to come before you and help you here, as perhaps you have covenanted with some dear sister or brother still waiting.

And even though in this life I am older, I am your sister, too. And I love you and know that on the other side we were all the same age. We all shared in great love and sisterhood for each other.

Yes, there is joy in motherhood and sisterhood! And it is a joy that will extend far into the eternal world to come.

Not everyone will have children in this life. Some will never marry, some will not be able to have children. This does not mean there is no joy in motherhood for those girls!

Satan would have us believe that, so that our self-esteem would suffer.

We will *all* be joyful mothers. The Lord has promised that to those who are faithful to the end. Those who do not skip any of the steps to celestial marriage (even if it means not marrying) will become the mothers of multitudes—the mothers of spirits without number. He promised. He is God and cannot break His promises. But we must keep our part of the bargain.

We must prepare to be mothers by being chaste, clean, and obedient. This is the challenge I leave with you, my lovely young sisters. Never let the eternal perspective of motherhood dim from your view. Always read the roadmaps and stay on the roads that are clearly marked. Hang on to the vision of yourself as a Mother in Heaven with multitudes of children at your knee. That vision will help keep you off forbidden roads. That vision will give you inspiration to prepare for motherhood, even if it does not come in this life. That vision will give you comfort and eternal perspective all of your life. That vision will indeed bring you joy!

JOY OF LOVE

"These things have I spoken unto you, that my joy might remain in you, and that your joy might be full. This is my commandment, That ye love one another, as I have loved you."

—John 15:11-12

What are the two greatest needs in every person's life?

To be loved.

To give love.

I asked Linda that question, and she could only answer number one. She made guesses at the second great need and missed it completely. Linda had not only missed the answer, she had missed something she was desperately lacking in her life. With all her thoughts turned inward, she had failed to see the second greatest need in her life, to give love.

We all want to be loved, to be of worth and value to others. But the most miserable people on the face of the whole earth are those who only recognize the need of being loved. The most miserable people I know are the ones who spend their whole lives looking for ways to bring love and attention to themselves. They are caught up in that whirlwind called "serving self." Everything they do is for themselves. They do not use their talents to help others. They look for what they can gain in a relationship, never what they can give. They blame others for their problems and mistakes. They are offended (or take things too personally) because their thoughts are only about themselves. They exist as if the whole world revolved around them. They are miserable because they never seem satisfied, never seem to be loved enough.

Those people truly are never satisfied, because they have missed another part of love—giving it to others. Why was Linda miserable? Remember her reasons?

- She had to wear braces on her teeth until she was fifteen.
- She had to save months of babysitting money to be able to afford one pair of designer jeans. Her parents could not afford to buy her the latest clothes.
- She was shy about making new friends.
- Her complexion was less than flawless.
- She struggled to keep up her math grades.
- She didn't get asked to the junior prom.
- She made some mistakes morally.
- She had confrontations with her parents.
- Her father criticized her often and pointed out her faults.
- She withdrew from her parents at times.
- She often said the wrong thing.
- She felt rules were "holding her back."
- She didn't make the swim team.
- She was puzzled by some gospel principles.

As she exercised the advice outlined in this book, she experienced joy. And one of the joys that came back into her life was love! As she loved herself more, she was able to love others more, too. As she loved others, she began to serve them. As she served them, she began to grow in sisterhood with her friends, neighbors, and loved ones. She began to enjoy people like she never thought possible. She was charming and pleasant and delightful to be around.

Then guess what happened? People began loving to be around her! And soon Linda found she was loved and needed in life.

I told you who the most miserable people in the world are. Now let me tell you about some of the happiest people I know. They are not rich or famous. In fact, they are a lot like you. Some of them even have some severe problems and trials in life. But they are happy people who have great self-esteem. They know the joy of love because they have learned to *give love* first. They are:

A lovely young lady who was so severely burned in her teens that she was left completely blind and without much of a face. She now spends much of her time singing to children confined to hospital beds, some who are even dying. She sings like an angel and is developing this talent to give love and happiness to others.

A pretty, popular senior in high school who was in all the school activities and was to be head cheerleader the coming school year. During the summer her father died suddenly, leaving her mother without much money to care for the family of seven young children. She saw her mother struggle to hold down two jobs and worry about the care of her home and children. All on her own she went to her mother and said, "Mother, I have decided to finish my last year of high school at night so I can stay home and take care of the house and children for you." This sweet and happy girl sacrificed all her own honors and pleasures because she understood the true joy of love.

Three happy sixteen-year-old girls who give up *every* Saturday morning to clean the home of a woman who has multiple sclerosis and cannot care for her family. No one asked them; they saw a need and went to help—no, they went to *love*. They spend two hours early every Saturday morning and even do her laundry. They know the true joy of love.

A twenty-three-year-old friend of mine who was a ski champion was training for the U.S. Olympic Ski Team. She had a diving accident the summer (at age seventeen) before the trials that severed her spinal cord and left her paralyzed from the neck down. And where is she now? What is left of her self-esteem? Can there be any joy for her? She is a therapist for paraplegics in a West Coast rehabilitation clinic. Although she is unable to help with physical exercise, she counsels, encourages, and inspires the people in her same condition. She is a success because she *loves* them. And do you know what? They love her, too! Her happy smile and dancing eyes tell you she knows the real joy of love!

Then there is the example of our beloved Prophet, Spencer W. Kimball. Several years ago he and Sister Kimball were invited to a dinner at the BYU President's home. Many of the faculty and staff were present. President and Sister Kimball arrived in a car, driven by a chauffeur, because the President doesn't drive anymore. The chauffeur parked and waited in the car.

After all the greetings were over, everyone stepped aside so President and Sister Kimball could serve themselves first. An observer said he watched with anticipation what the Prophet would choose; he'd heard the Prophet didn't eat much.

Sister Kimball went first, and then the President came, plate in hand, silverware tucked under it, and a roll in his forearm. He piled the plate higher and higher. Then carefully balancing it all including a glass of punch, he guided Camilla to her seat. The others present saw pure love. The prophet of God went out the front door, down the walk, and served the chauffeur first!

There are lots of happy young women everywhere who have caught the meaning of the joy of love. Where did they start? Right in their own homes, by loving their parents and obeying them. They found great self-esteem in serving and loving others.

Satan's most popular wedge between the Lord and His people has been his idea, "DO YOUR OWN THING." Satan means to turn our thoughts to ourselves. Selfish people are not like God or Jesus Christ. Satan is selfish. Remember, he wanted all the glory for himself.

The Lord knew this would happen in the last days so He warned us:

> he that findeth his life shall lose it; and he that loseth his life for my sake shall find it. (Matthew 10:39.)

"Finding yourself" today seems to mean to serve yourself, to do your own thing. The Lord warned that those who do that will "lose" their lives, meaning they won't really find the life they want. For them there will be no real joy. But those who "lose" their lives for the Lord's sake, He promised, would truly "find themselves." He means those people will know the true meaning of the joy of love.

What is His sake? What does it mean to "lose" ourselves for Him?

> These things have I spoken unto you, that my joy might remain in you, and that your joy might be full. This is my commandment, That ye love one another, as I have loved you. (John 15:11-12.)

BEHOLD MY JOY IS FULL

So there you have it, ten JOYS of life, ten JOYS of self-esteem, ten beautiful gospel principles that will bring you closer to the person you want to become!

Linda knows.

Linda recently wrote:

> I know the thing that helped my self-esteem the most as a teenager was the gospel. Yet, I ignored that so often. When I lived the gospel, I felt good about myself. When I didn't follow the teachings, I spent a great deal of my time in self-criticism or self-hatred or just plain selfishness!
>
> If you live the gospel, you will have self-esteem. I see how this concept affects my whole life and how it has affected my life in the past.
>
> But I know I can't dwell on my past mistakes. I know I need to keep going and learning.
>
> As I have learned to pray, I have felt closer to Heavenly Father. That makes me want to obey Him more. That has given me greater powers to have more self-control.
>
> More self-control has made me realize how much better I am than I thought I was and that has made me try harder. I have worked harder in school and set better goals and made definite plans for my life.
>
> I have also found peace in repentance and am thankful for Jesus who died on the cross for me. I want to live so He will know I appreciate what He did. That has helped me share my testimony with others, and sharing my testimony with others has made it stronger. My best friend even took the lessons and was baptized. I have learned that giving love is better than getting it!
>
> But, Anita, the things that used to bother me real bad don't hurt so much anymore. As I have learned to follow the gospel, I have found I can handle my problems and trials, too. And I realize *everybody* has them.

I am so glad to be alive! I am so thankful to Heavenly Father for giving me this chance to be on earth! I am so happy and so blessed to be a member of the true Church. I am so glad to be a woman, and I want to be just like my Heavenly Mother.

Anita, my joy *is* full!

Is that a different Linda than the one who came to see me one year ago? It certainly is! Linda is on her way to her eternal destiny. She has caught the vision of Eternal Perspective.

Sow a thought, reap an act;
Sow an act, reap a habit;
Sow a habit, reap a character;
Sow a character, reap an eternal destiny.

—Anonymous

Linda once thought that her life was like a book with blank pages. She thought that until lots of accomplishments were written on those pages she would not be worth much. She had to re-learn how wrong that idea is. We are worth a great deal just because we exist! We have done *nothing* to earn Heavenly Father's love. We have it already because we are His daughters. He loves us for that reason alone! We don't always have His approval, but we always have His love!

I want to tell you, each and every one of you, that you are well acquainted with God our Heavenly Father . . . for there is not a soul of you but what has lived in his house and dwelt with him year after year; and yet you are seeking to become acquainted with him, when the fact is, you have merely forgotten what you did know. There is not a person here today but what is a son or a daughter of that Being.

—Discourses of Brigham Young

Knowing who we are gives us purpose in life. Experiencing the ten joys in this book will help you be more secure in who you are. You will face your three great concerns in life with greater confidence:

•What is my purpose in life?

- Who will I marry?
- How do I gain a testimony?

You will be able to tackle all three with greater understanding and eternal perspective.

Imagine yourself with us in the preexistence, in our Heavenly Home. It will aid you in your quest for eternal perspective. Imagine with Steve and I as we prepared for our birth into this life:

Dear Steven,

It seems like eternities since I've seen you, but it's only been a week today. I hope my letter finds you busily engaged in your studies at the University of Kolob. I can hardly believe so many eons of time have passed, and we only have about 1900 years to prepare for mortality. The prospect of earth life is exciting, although I must admit some fear at the thought of the veil being drawn. I worry sometimes that we won't find each other, or, even worse, that I won't remember all I am learning here.

Speaking of learning—it is so exciting to be enrolled this millenium here at the Institute. So many of the classes are being taught by Mother Herself. Oh, how I want to be just like her and Father.

I could write all night, but I must make this letter short since I have an exam to study for in the morning, but I wanted to reconfirm our meeting place in two weeks on Thursday. Since Father has called upon all the Hosts of Heaven to witness this great event, I'm afraid we may not find each other in the crowd at the Great Assembly Hall.

It will be such a privilege to share this sacred time with you. It brings to memory the other wonderful experience we shared just 33 years ago when we sang in the choir on the eve of our Elder Brother's birth.

I know that Thursday and Friday will be trying hours for Him, but I am so excited to see Him again. I love Him so much.

Well, I must close. Please write soon and tell me where to

meet you.

With love,
Anita

Dear Anita,

It was so good to hear from you again. I miss our long walks and tender moments together. I don't want you to be afraid of the veil. We both want to become like Father and Mother, and the only way we can is to go through earth life as They did.

When I think of mortality, I think of great challenges to rise to. I am grateful to Father for the plan He presented to us. I am also grateful to our brother Jesus for the sacrifice He volunteered to make for everyone. I, too, am looking forward to the three important days of next week. Father has been admonishing us all to be in attendance for this great event—The Atonement. He says it will be a learning experience for us all. I am not fully sure of what he means or what more information we will gain, but it will be nice to share it with you. It will also be good to reunite with many of our friends, especially those whom have been reserved like us to be born in the last days of the earth.

I have some exciting news to tell you. Today Father fore-ordained me to hold the Holy Priesthood after the order of the Son of God. What a blessing and opportunity! I covenanted with Him that I would remain true and faithful. I intend to keep that covenant. I will meet you at an early hour, say twelve noon, so we won't miss a single event. Meet me at the fountains by the tenth column.

With love,
Steve

Dear Steve,

I love that particular fountain by the tenth column, and I shall meet you at twelve noon promptly.

I have been thinking a lot about the Atonement lately, and

what it will mean to me personally. I am not sure I comprehend the total picture yet either . . .

I can remember back to the Council in Heaven when Father presented His plan, and Satan and Jesus came forth—Satan to alter the plan and Jesus to uphold it. It is still clear in my mind, as if it were just yesterday, the awful war that followed. I remember vividly the burning in my heart as my name was called, and I stepped forward to be counted on the Lord's side. My heart still pounds, but then aches as I see many who also stepped forward that day but have lost their way after they were born into mortality. It could easily happen to any of us if we aren't careful.

I can see how perfect Father's plan is. He has provided a Savior who will pay for the sins that have been or ever will be committed, and I see that includes me. What a swelling in my heart it brings to know this, to know how much They love me and want me back. I feel great comfort despite the knowledge of the veil, that repentance on Jesus' name will be a miracle and a blessing.

I hope that after this week's events, I will more fully comprehend His mission on earth and The Atonement. Looking forward to seeing you,

With love,
Anita

Dear Anita,

I hope this letter arrives before we meet on Thursday. I can hardly wait to be with you and discuss the atonement in depth and then experience it together. I, too, have been thinking about what it will mean to me personally. The greatest fact of all is that I can become as Father is. That is, unspotted and pure with a body of flesh and bones. The resurrection is supposed to make the spirit and body eternal somehow. It is thrilling to see how the Savior really is one with the Father. That is my goal, too. I know we can make it! If we listen to the third member of the Godhead, the Holy Ghost, after we come to earth. I know we'll be able to recognize the truth from the evil because when we hear the truth, it will ring a familiar chord, and the burning you spoke of will be there in our hearts. So you see, Anita, the veil is not all that thick. Just remember to pay attention . . . you'll know. I must close to get this off right away. See you in two days.

With love,
Steve

Dear Steve,

It has been two weeks now since we knelt and wept together with all our brothers and sisters. I have not been able to write until now because of the deep emotion I have felt. I never imagined the Crucifixion and Resurrection could have been so spiritually and intellectually moving.

I truly did learn more during those three days than I have in all my existence. The poignant scene of His last supper with His Disciples opened a new understanding for me. I saw it did for you, too, as we wept together for the messages there.

Can you imagine how our Brother felt? Knowing of the impending hour, the mockery, the torture, and pain He must surely suffer. Can you imagine how heavy those hours must have been upon Him? It was so touching to watch Him with His dear friends gathered there in that supper room—His apostles, men He had lived with and been a constant companion to for all His ministry. These were His choice—His annointed. They must carry on after Him. It was so hard for Him to bid farewell. He loved them so much. Wasn't it beautiful the way He tenderly embraced each one and spent a few private moments individually to express His love and appreciation personally—one-to-one?

I could not hold back the tears as I saw Him—The Great Jehovah—our Lord—our Master—the Savior of the world—get down upon his knees with no thoughts of His coming ordeal and lovingly wash each apostle's feet. My heart and mind will never forget what He said:

"A new commandment I give unto you, *That ye love one another as I have loved you.* By this shall all men know that ye are my disciples, *if* ye have love one to another."

At that moment I knew He wasn't talking to His apostles alone. He was talking to all of us. At that moment I realized that the withholding of love is the negation of the Spirit of Christ, the proof that we never knew Him, that for us He lived in vain. It means He suggested nothing in all our thoughts, that He inspired nothing in all our lives.

At that moment I covenanted when it was my turn, when I go down to mortality, I shall live my life so His would not have been in vain. I would love others as He loved me. I do know Him. I think everyone present made that covenant, don't you? There was an overwhelming feeling there as the Heavens were silent, and everyone felt the majesty of our Lord Jesus Christ. Becoming like Father, Mother, and Jesus is love. I now see what is meant by GOD IS LOVE.

My heart ached and grieved as I witnessed Him bleed from every pore at Gethsemane. I have never before seen such a thing happen. At first I didn't understand. I thought the sins weighing upon him were causing all the suffering. Then I recognized that He was also experiencing great sorrow, that which I have seen accompanies sin. The remorse felt *after* the sin has been committed. I saw my Lord suffer that great sorrow multiplied uncountable times. Even though I am yet unborn, I know my sins were numbered there, too, and I caused some of that pain. And yet I could take hope and not condemn myself because *I realized I am worth the price He paid or He would not have paid it.* We are all worth it. It causes me to sense how much we should esteem one another, especially those who have lost their way. I never understood until now why He told the story of the joy of finding the one lost sheep while 99 were safe. I know I am weak, too, Steve, in so many areas. If I lose my way, I can now clearly see the road home, and it is stained with His blood. I love Him for that.

I could hardly watch as they scourged and flogged Him. The cruel whip laced with bits of bone and glass tore open His flesh, and I wished they would stop. With every mocking word and gashing blow, my heart would reconfirm my covenant—"I will love you, my Savior, and try so hard to remember who I am."

As they drove the nails into His hands and wrists and feet, I can remember thinking of the blood everywhere, from Gethsemane, to the beatings, and then on the cross. He literally gave most of His own blood for us.

As He hung there and the choir here softly hummed a hallowed song, I turned to see Father and Mother. They suffered, too. The look on their faces was similar to the one on Mary's, and yet there was peace about them. They knew, they knew what that moment meant to the worlds.

Steve, my closest brother, that you are, promise me you will help me and that you will honor the Priesthood you have been foreordained to receive. I promise I will help you. We must all help one another to love, honor, and obey the Father and the Son so that we can one day come back home.

Love,
Your sister, Anita

Dear Anita,

Your letter so vividly described my exact feelings as I knelt with you that day. There was not a soul present who could not have felt that spiritual awakening within. The tears flowed freely. As our Lord hung on the cross, He had the power to take His life at any moment. Seeing Him in such agony, I wanted Him to finish it. My honor for Him was highest of all as I realized He would allow himself the suffering until it was finished. Do you recall when he said, "My God, my God, why hast thou forsaken me?" All during the ordeal, even though He was half God, He needed Father there with Him to help Him through it. Father was there at the supper, Gethsemane, the trial, the beating, and up to the moment He cried out with such woe. I realized that Father at that moment on the cross had withdrawn His spirit. Why? I thought it was harsh. I then came to the realization as I looked over into Father's face. He loved His son so dearly He wanted Him to share in the glory, too. He wanted Him to go a little way all alone, so our Brother would feel and share in the glory, too. How loving, how noble of our omnipotent Father. So great is His love for us. So you see, Anita, so many of our brothers and sisters who have gone to mortality and think He's forgotten them just aren't listening. He will let us go a little way on our own sometimes so that we can share in the glory, too. Don't you think it will be a great day to come home, meet Him, embrace Him, and say, "Father, I did it! I endured to the end, and now I am home." What glory for us that will be.

What a privilege it was to watch the Savior open the mission to the spirit prison those three days between His crucifixion and resurrection. Everyone will have the chance to accept or reject the Gospel of Jesus Christ. Anita, a lot of this work will be up to you and me. It is an awesome responsibility, this temple work and genealogy. We can't let our Brother down.

But I guess the most glorious sight I shall ever behold, until perhaps the Second Coming, was to see Him rise body and spirit united *forever and eternally from the grave!* As you and I knelt there together, I felt the power of what the moment meant. Suddenly the words *faith, repentance, baptism,* and the *gift of the Holy Ghost* took on new meaning. Faith in our Brother our Redeemer and in Father *and in ourselves.* Repentance, the key to unlock misery and forgiveness through His name whose blood we saw shed. Baptism for the remission of sins so that we can hold the keys to become like Him and the gift of the Holy Ghost to guide us and help us along the way.

I do promise to find you, Father allowing, and you must help me, too. But don't forget our Savior's words, "My sheep hear my voice and I know them, and they follow me." Remember, it will be through the power of the Holy Ghost that we will re-remember these days and hours here. He will make it all seem familiar to us.

On Sunday His final days on earth with His disciples are finished, and He will be coming home. I shall again meet you at our regular meeting place to welcome Him home.

It will be a glorious morning. The choirs are assembling, the heavens will be thunderous with music and hosannas. Father and Mother have made great preparations. The finest of foods and vessels and flowers and adornment are being made ready. The glory will be bursting!

But I look most forward to the moments we will each be able to spend with Him and thank Him and embrace Him. It will be so wonderful to personally express my love to Him and share my excitement that we, His brothers and sisters, can become just like Him! He marked the roads and led the way, because He believes in us. He knows we can do it. I love Him for that confidence in us.

I look forward to seeing you again and being able to bear witness of the truth of all these things.

With love,
Your brother, Steve

Never lose that eternal perspective. Picture yourself in a beautiful white flowing robe among your Heavenly Parents, friends, and family. Decide and plan on being there, and you will make it!

It is while you are standing undecided, uncommitted, and self-serving that you will be an easy target for Satan. He wants to destroy you so that you will never have joy.

You must stand firm and decide to take charge of your life. You must try to make correct choices in order to enhance your natural talents and abilities. Doing this will bring you closer to the true joy you seek:

Joy in life
Joy in the Lord
Joy in the heart
Joy in being a righteous young woman

> To be a righteous (young) woman is a glorious thing in any age. To be a righteous (young) woman in the winding up scenes of this earth before the Second Coming of our Savior is an especially noble calling. The righteous (young) woman's strength and influence today can be tenfold what it might be in more tranquil times. (Spencer W. Kimball, *My Beloved Sisters*, p. 17. Parenthetical expressions added.)

These are the winding up scenes before the Lord's coming. We have some tight places to go before the Lord is through with us and this Church. In this day of free love, abortion, lewdness, open sex, lesbianism, disinterest in the home—there is a steady beam of light through the darkness—it is *you*, my lovely sisters! The world hardly knows that such nobler young women exist. Young women who are prayerful, obedient, chaste, industrious, intelligent, spiritual, honorable. Young women who love others, serve others, have compassion for others; young women who love the Lord.

Your eternal joy is now in the making. Those feelings and desires you have in your heart for excellence and success have been planted there to help you reach your destiny and have true joy!

Your joy lies within you. You have the power to obtain it and keep it. Your joy lies in:

- Sincere Prayer
- Hard Work
- Planned Education
- The Companionship of the Holy Ghost
- Missionary Work to Your Friends
- The Miracle of Repentance
- The Pain and Joy of Bittersweet Trials

•Preparation for Motherhood
•Love and Service to Others

Doing these things will bring great joy. The joy that comes from self-worth and self-esteem—in knowing who you are. I promise you that.

But even so, even in living a full and happy life, the Lord has told us that if we are faithful to the end, no one can even begin to imagine how great our joy in eternity will be:

> Wherefore, fear not even unto death; for in this world your joy is not full, but in me your joy is full. (D&C 101:36.)

Living with our Redeemer and Savior is the joy I seek. Don't you?

What is joy?

Joy is to know who we are.
Joy is to know things that God knows.
Joy is to possess what He possesses.
Joy is to be like Him and live with Him.
Joy is to be a queen, a Priestess, and a Goddess forever and ever and ever.

Dear sweet, lovely, young friends and sisters, read your roadmaps, stay away from unmarked roads. Hold on to eternal perspective. Hold in your hearts always that great eternal moment when the hour comes to meet Him face to face. Oh, yes, our JOY will be full! And, hold in your hearts the look on His face when He welcomes you Home and tells *you,*

"Sweet little Daughter, Behold *My* Joy is full to have you Home!"